Cavegirl Cuisine

eating paleo... one bone at a time!

Recipes for the Paleo & Gluten-Free Lifestyle

written and photographed by Michelle Fagone

SUNNY DAY®
PUBLISHING, LLC
a health education company™

Cover Design by One2One Solutions
Interior Design by Stacie Gerrity

Printed in the United States of America

Sunny Day Publishing, LLC
www.sunnydaypublishing.com

ISBN 978-0-9825480-8-0

SUNNY DAY®
PUBLISHING, LLC
a health education company™

This cookbook is dedicated to
the wonderfully functional group of insanity
that I call my family.
Thank you for loving me right back.

Table of Contents

Table of Contents

Forward

When Michelle approached us about writing a foreword for her book, we were a little star-struck, but honored to comply. She said, "I actually decided to do a cookbook because of something James (from FastPaleo.com) told me early on in an email. He said that he would write the foreword to my cookbook. I thought he was crazy, but he planted the seed."

Known as the pony-tailed Cavegirl Cuisine on Facebook and her website, she has established quite a presence in the online paleo community, and is known and loved by thousands. Whatever she touches turns to gold, or better, whatever foods she experiments with, turns into fabulous paleo recipes.

She has created much-loved traditional comfort foods, but doesn't shy away from new challenges either. What does one do with an ostrich egg? Do chicken and waffles mix? Would dragon fruit make good vinaigrette? She's been an avid cook since childhood, learning to follow recipes from her mom, and then un-follow them from her dad. There seems to be no end to her creativity, and the results are usually amazing. It seems only natural that the next step for her would be to write a cookbook, a compilation of all the greatest recipes she's created.

We've tried several of Michelle's recipes ourselves, and they're always a hit with friends and family. And her Cinnamon Ice Cream is quite simply to die for.

Michelle has uploaded countless recipes to FastPaleo.com to share with the world, and we always look forward to find out what new and tasty creation she has come up with. Michelle makes paleo living easy and enjoyable. We love working with her. She is super friendly, well-read, smart, and witty. Cross Fitting, mothering, and cooking... Michelle makes it look easy. We can only imagine where this powerhouse of a woman is going, and we're excited to follow her on this great journey.

Someday we hope to pass through Louisville and meet her and her lovely family in person and enjoy a good paleo meal together.

James Gregory, Owner & Operator
Ute Mitchell, Operations Manager
FastPaleo.com— Paleo Recipe Sharing Site

Acknowledgements

To Samantha and Calla ~ My two crazy, wonderful daughters; My world completely flipped when you two entered my life, and I wouldn't change a thing. Thank you for all of the photo angle input and your beautiful creative eyes! All my heart, Mom

To Sam ~ My linear thinking, Spock-like, handsome husband... Thank you for always letting me live in the gray, chase my dreams and just be me... and for being such a willing and supportive taste-tester! I love you forever.

To Mom and Dad ~ Thank you for all of the adventures around the world! Dad, thank you for giving me the desire to try new things and be unabashed about it! Mom, thank you for always being my moral compass, but laughing with me when I go off-track.

To Laura ~ From one only child to another... We ARE special (just ask us)! Thanks for being my friend forever and my designated driver when there is a karaoke machine within a mile of me. Here is another cookbook for your collection... Sarah and Emma will appreciate it!

To Cathy K ~ You have taught me to not take myself so seriously and to tackle any project with reckless abandon. Thank you for always having solutions and not just problems... It's a rare and admirable trait!

To my Facebook and blog friends ~ Thank you for the laughs, advice, questions, and constant support. Without you, none of this would have been possible!

To Linda at One2One Solutions ~ Thank you, thank you, thank you for having the uncanny ability to read my mind. Cheers!

To Mayra, Pam, and Stacie at Sunny Day Publishing ~ Thank you for taking a chance on me and being such an incredibly supportive group of wonderful women!

Taste Testers (thank you!)

Alita B.
Amber Bean, PaleoSavvy
Amy Ayers
April and June Cho Paik
Camille Gonzalez Mami
Cara Cicalese Flaherty
Carolina
Christine E. Crouse-Dick
Cindy Hagen
Deanna Reynolds
Debbie Winebrenner
Donna Jones
Ellen Puetz
Gina Giggey
Gina Paige
Heather Earnhardt
Jean Bentz

Jennifer Wyatt, "That Paleo Gal"
Judith Dore
Kal Buckles
Kate Koger
Kathy Heidebrecht
Katrina B.
Kerry Moore Spencer
Laura Darr
Leah Barkhuff
Leona Kealey Vamos
Lindsey Canaley
Lisa Stock
Lori Borenstein
Maria Regner
Marjorie Maske
Mary Michela
Meghan M. Kiely
Mike Gorman

Rebecca Benton
Robbin Byrne Goodskey
Sandee McDaniel
Sandi B.
Scott & Karen Burg
Stacey Rothchild
Stephani Bayhylle
Stephanie K. Lewis
Sue Flanagan
Suzanne M.
Tara Sotelo
Taryn Neva
Vicki C. White
Suzanne M.
Tara Sotelo
Taryn Neva
Vicki C. White

What is Paleo?

"Paleo" refers to the Paleolithic Era, or the "cavegirl" days. It was coined "paleo" to remind us to eat like our ancestors did; in a time before industrialized farming practices put their hands on our food supply. In a nutshell, the goal is to eliminate grains, dairy, sugar, beans (legumes) and anything processed. Yes, this includes artificial sweeteners, as well. Those who choose paleo strive to consume antibiotic-free meats, from grassfed and free-roaming animals, lots of veggies, fruits, nuts, seeds, animal fats, and certain "beneficial" oils, for instance coconut oil, for cooking and food preparation.

The next time you purchase a packaged food that makes such "healthy" claims as fat-free, heart-healthy, added fiber and the like, flip the box over and read the ingredients. Most importantly, look at the grams of sugar or carbohydrates. When one item is eliminated, such as fat, another is added to replace it. Fat is replaced by sugar in these "low fat" items. However, fat does not make us fat… sugar does. It's a good practice to start reading labels. Almost everything includes sugar… down to your ketchup.

Many times, someone would ask, "Then what can I eat?"— I started my blog, Cavegirl Cuisine.com, to answer these types of questions. I decided to cook from the paleo-recommended list of ingredients and created my own recipes. The twist... I modified versions of the traditional foods, that we all grew up with, and "paleo-fied" them. The answer was, "There is a LOT that you can eat!!!" Not only can you eat it but the modified recipes turned out to be DELICIOUS!

Although there seems to be many restrictions… no dairy, no beans, no bread… one must also take into account their personal trials. They should consider allergies to dairy, nuts, and/or nightshades. Please, use these recipes as a guide and hopefully an inspiration to create your own traditions.

Note: You will not see any cheese in my recipes, but there are some recipes that lend themselves to this addition. So, if every now and then you want to make a recipe with a little cheese, go for it, if your stomach can handle it. My suggestion would be to source a local, fresh cheese that is minimally processed.

eating paleo... one bone at a time!

Why Paleo?

My trainer, Lauren Dawson, first introduced "paleo" to me. Prior to that, I had been "eating clean" for about a year. The first time she mentioned this new way of eating to me, it seemed a little extreme; no sugar, dairy, whole grains or beans? Just another diet, I thought. But curiosity always gets the best of me. Therefore, I couldn't help but to research this lifestyle.

A friend of mine convinced me to sign up for a "28-day Nutritional Paleo Course", at Maximum Fitness/Black Label CrossFit®, in Mt. Washington, Kentucky. Kyle Harrod, the owner, was our speaker and mentor. His passion for this lifestyle inspired me to learn more. The stories from the other participants were compelling. One lady had completed the 28-day course at a prior date and the pain in her knees from arthritis disappeared. She stated, that in between courses, she went back to eating like she used to and the pain came back. This is when I started reading about inflammation and the Standard American Diet (SAD). What were we being taught? Why were we being taught that this pyramid of foods was the right way to eat?

I started my journey slowly, but eagerly. Processed foods went out the door. They were no longer an option, in our house. It had already been about a year and half since I had eaten a fast food "slime burger", but I learned new terms like "local", "grass-fed", and "non-GMO". I started reading about different cooking oils and smoke points, along with different choices, such as, avocado oil, coconut oil, and almond oil. The staples in my pantry started shifting from all-purpose flour and spelt flour over to coconut flour and almond meal. These changes did not happen overnight, but they did happen. My weight dropped, my skin was more clear, my stamina was up, and my sleep was really sound.

There's a lot of science behind the "whys" of this way of eating; however, I will leave this to the scientists and trailblazers. I just like to cook. Over the past few years, I have learned a new way to cook. I have watched my husband and children change their eating habits, slowly at times, but there is change, nonetheless. My girls are asking questions, learning how to round out their meals and snacks and are just all-together curious about how food affects their bodies. Raising two young happy and healthy women, who are aware of what they eat, instead of obsessing over their body image, is my ultimate goal as a mom.

Saturday mornings are my favorite! Going to the local farmer's market is something I look forward to all week. The fresh eggs, local meats, colorful fruits, and veggies… I feel alive around the freshness, tie-dye shirts, and homemade soaps. My formal education is business (Bachelors in Marketing and a Masters in Human Relations). However, my inner "hippie-chic" comes alive on these days at the farmer's market. Each week I try new things. (Yes, I knew what rainbow chard was… but I had never cooked with it). Fresh rabbit? Sure, why not. These new-to-me ingredients made me feel so energized and alive in the kitchen. It's as if it woke the inner-chef in me! The Internet made much of this possible. I picked something that looked new and interesting. I "searched" a recipe, and an hour or two later, we enjoyed my masterpiece. (Sometimes, I would even giggle a little, to myself, with pleasure at my sense of accomplishment).

Why Paleo? (continued)

On March 5, 2012 I decided to start a blog. I wasn't sure how this would work, but I really wanted to share my recipes. I wanted others to have fun in the kitchen, with me. I started going to farmer's markets and trying everything. I would take my girls to the produce section of our local "healthy" grocery store and tell them to go find something that they had never tried. We would go home and look up recipes on the Internet, with these ingredients. Then, we would try to come up with our own versions. I was, and still am, so proud of their adventurous spirits. They may not like everything, but they do give it the "one-bite try". Seven times out of ten, they like it! They even tried pickled octopus one time and both actually liked it ~ suction cups and all ~ LOL!

After a few months, my blog (cavegirlcuisine.com) and Facebook page really seemed to take off. The support of the readers and this community is amazing. The input that I have received is invaluable. The laughs I get from the feedback are amazing. The lift I get when someone loves and shares a recipe is huge (I'm an only child... Praise is a requirement of life for our type)!

This cookbook houses recipes that represent the past year of my life and my blog with many extra never-before-seen recipes. I never imagined how this journey would have changed me on that morning on March 5th when I was sitting at my kitchen counter trying to come up with a name for my site. I really, really wanted to be Captain Cavegirl ~ said in Mel Blanc's voice of "Captain Caveeeemannn!!" But, that domain name was taken and I feel like fate intervened and led me to my Internet "home", Cavegirl Cuisine.

My hope is that you enjoy these recipes and aren't afraid to not only try new things, but make these recipes your very own. Put your own stamp on it. If the recipe calls for onions and you don't like onions, by all means, leave them out. Substitute bell peppers, if you'd prefer. If you don't like maple syrup, then substitute raw honey. If you are lactose-intolerant and one of my soups calls for some organic heavy cream, don't put it in. You know you. You know your intolerances and your preferences. Believe what your body is telling you. Do your research. Make good choices. Buy local as much as possible. Have fun in the kitchen. These are the simple rules that I live by. Also, if you eat a piece of crusty bread or have a few glasses of wine ~ who cares!!! You didn't fall off the wagon; you were just living your life. Wake up tomorrow and make better choices.

Happy Eating!

Michelle Fagone

"Cavegirl Cuisine"

Kitchen and Pantry Makeover

Let me start by saying that my kitchen did not get a facelift overnight. This was a process that evolved over months of cooking and learning and experimenting. So, please don't get overwhelmed by the list below. These items are just my way of explaining some ingredients and kitchen tools that help me to eat the "paleo" way.

Also, take your time. For instance, start by tossing out your refined sugars and artificial sweeteners. Explore other sweeteners such as, local honey, maple syrup, and coconut crystals... the list goes on! Next, introduce yourself to nut flours and get rid of that all-purpose flour. Just have fun with the process and experiment with new foods and start listening to the dialogue of your body.

Note: If there is something on this list that you personally don't like, eat or use, then skip it... no biggie. Everyone's journey is a personal one.

Almond Meal/Flour ~ Almond flour and almond meal are used in many paleo recipes. They are really interchangeable, with just a slight difference. Almond flour is finer than meal. Also, these are such easy items to make. I buy raw, unsalted almonds and process them in my food processor (just process longer for the flour). I store two separate containers in my pantry. You will find that you will have a preference for one or the other in different recipes.

Bacon Grease ~ Our grandmas weren't so off their rocker by saving bacon grease. Let the grease cool a little and then strain it into your bacon grease container. The straining will help sort out those extra little bacon bits that can cause your grease to go rancid. I also like to use bacon grease to season my cast-iron skillet.

Cast-Iron Skillet ~ Take a step back in time and bring back your grandma's cast-iron pan. She was on to something. Using a cast-iron pan actually leaches some iron into your food while cooking!

Coconut Aminos ~ This is used as a soy sauce or tamari substitute. It's great as a dipping sauce and even better in vinaigrettes and marinades!

Coconut Milk ~ If you like ice cream or ice pops, keep a few cans of this in your pantry. It can generally be found in the international aisle of your grocer. It may become one of your staples. Also, it's great in Thai soups and Caribbean fish dishes.

Coconut Oil ~ This is a great staple to keep around. Not only is it great when cooking at high-temperatures because of its stability, but also works wonders on your skin (and smells great to boot)! For greasing a pan, because coconut oil is solid at room temperature, just melt a little and use a pastry brush to spread a thin coat over your baking pan.

CSA ~ This stands for "community supported agriculture". Look it up ~ I bet there is one in your area! Basically, you choose your pick-up point and once a week you are given a box of what has been harvested at area farms. It's a wonderful way to try new items, eat fresh food, and support your local farmers.

Cutting Board ~ I can never have enough cutting boards. I have big beautiful wooden ones down to my little plastic cutting boards. Just make sure you clean and care for them. It is a preference thing, but I generally cut meats on a plastic cutting board so that I can throw it in the dishwasher to take advantage of the high heat cleaning. I use my main wooden cutting board for prepping the remaining mise en place, or set up prior to cooking.

Dutch Oven ~ This is a heavy pot that has become one of my main kitchen staples. Once purchased to make Dutch Oven Bread, it now serves a new purpose. I use this pot to cook my whole chicken, once a week. I then transfer it to the stovetop and make my broth. From there, I use the broth to make a soup. It's a resilient piece of kitchenware that has become invaluable. My MVP in the kitchen, for sure!

Farmer's Market ~ Most cities have a version of a farmer's market. When I lived in the St. Louis Metro area, I would visit Soulard's Farmer's Market... it was partially covered. It was definitely a well-oiled machine. I have often stopped alongside the road in Georgia (my home state) to buy fresh peaches or a fresh watermelon (the smallest version of a farmer's market, in my opinion, but it still qualifies). Somewhere, in between, is where most of us fall. You can buy fresh flowers, artisan cheeses, fresh seasonal produce, grass-fed meats, and eggs; but most importantly, you support your local farmer. Find your local farmer's market, tote along your favorite basket, and fill it with love!

Food Processor ~ A food processor is needed, not only to grind a variety of nuts for flours, but also great for pesto's, and more! I actually have a large one and a small one for little jobs. Either way, this is a great investment.

Ghee ~ Clarified butter that has been boiled to remove the milk solids and residue. It has a high smoke point, so it's a great option when baking.

Grill ~ Whether it's an outdoor grill, electric grilling appliance, or a grilling pan for your stovetop, learn to grill. Grilling your meat, for the week, on your prep day, really helps you stay on track.

Immersion Blender ~ Soups became a staple in our house, once I started cooking a chicken each week and making my own broth. My mom bought me an immersion blender for Christmas one year, and I've never looked back. Prior to this, I would transfer batches of my soup to a blender. Of course this worked. However, the mess level is much lower now that I can stick to one pot. The immersion blender is the best friend of a soup maker!

Knife Sharpener ~ The most dangerous kitchen utensil is a dull knife. Sharpen those knives... It will save the tips of your fingers.

Mandolin ~ If consistency in the cut is your thing, then you need a mandolin. This gizmo slices, dices, crinkle cuts, juliennes, and more.

Meat Thermometer ~ This changed my life. As you know fish and cuts of meat come in all sizes. One 5-ounce salmon fillet may be thicker and shorter than another 5-ounce piece of salmon, so there is really no absolute cooking time. I would end up cutting my meat/fish in half and "checking" it. There are a few problems with this. It is not pretty and it dries out your meal! Cooking meat to a desired internal temperature and then letting it rest for about five minutes helps the juices stay put, lending to a wonderfully moist steak, burger, chicken thigh, or piece of cod!

Nut Flour (see Almond Flour) ~ Use just about any nut you want to make your own flour. Currently, in my pantry, I have glass containers with hazelnut, pecan, and almond flour ready-to-go.

Parchment Paper ~ Once I discovered this, I never looked back! There are three wonderful benefits of using parchment. First, you don't have to "grease" your cookie sheet. Second, the only clean-up is throwing away the paper after baking. Third, have your ever cooked fish in a parchment paper pocket (en papillote)? You need to!

Professional Knives ~ Invest in a good set of knives. If you start out slowly, just buying one at a time, I would suggest getting a high-quality 8" chef's knife first. After that, a paring knife and a filet knife are perfect additions.

Slow Cooker ~ This is your new best friend; especially for the busy cooker… tell me, who is not too busy these days???

Vegetable Peeler ~ This is a fairly inexpensive yet necessary utensil. It is also great for making long curls for "vegetable pasta" if you don't have a spiraler. By the way, there are kid-friendly peelers on the market. It is a great tool to get the children in the kitchen!

Veggie Spiraler ~ LOVE! If you are tired of eating spaghetti squash all the time, as a substitute for pasta, then get a spiraler. Use it on your root veggies or squash of choice and add marinara. It creates anything from thin spirals to flat fettuccine-type "noodles".

Zester ~ This is a fairly inexpensive tool that can add a lot of flavor to many, many dishes. Zest limes, lemons, and oranges. The oil from the rind of citrus fruits is overlooked and often tossed away dismissing its remarkable flavor.

Prep Day

Pictured above:

diced red peppers
diced chicken
diced onions
seeded pomegranate
sliced mushrooms
hard-boiled eggs

This is just a start... depending on the season or your taste buds; prep what you use often in your dishes.

There are some mornings when I just want to stay in bed. On those days, I scramble an egg and add my pre-prepped items. My weekly prep saves me the "trouble" of chopping ingredients each day. The convenience of having my peppers, onions, mushrooms, chicken chopped/cubed, makes for an easy and healthy breakfast.

Hard-boiled eggs are a great on-the-go snack. They are great sliced, with my lunch, too.

My girls adore snacking on pomegranate seeds. My husband and I enjoy them on our salads.

This prep work can also assist in a quick soup, salad, and side dish. Use your imagination. The possibilities are endless!

Enjoy!

Breakfast

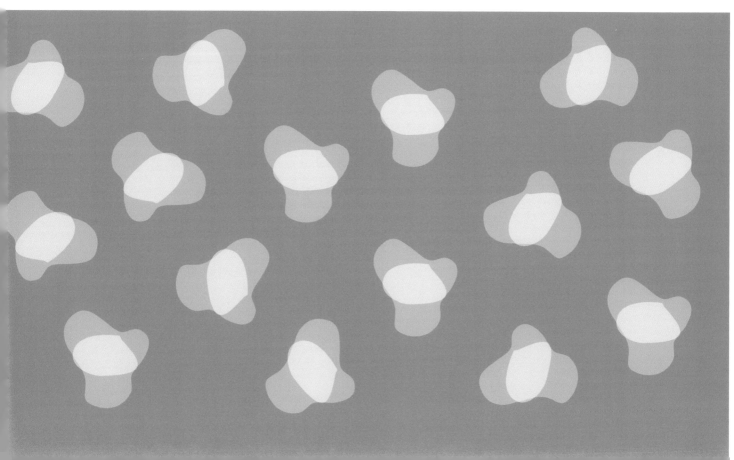

Breakfast

Sweet Potato Pancakes with Blueberry Maple Butter	19
Chocolate Dipped Doughnut Holes	20
Nutty Orangeberry Breakfast Muffins	21
Chocolate Waffles with Raspberry Maple Syrup	22
Maple Sage Breakfast Sausage (bulk)	23
Breakfast Casserole	24
2-Egg Omelette	25
Reuben Benedict	26
Eggstraordinary Lox Benedict	27
Paleo Honey Crunches Cereal	28
Choco-Hazelnut Paleo Cereal	29
Noatmeal	30

Sweet Potato Pancakes
with Blueberry Maple Butter

Syrup:
2 tablespoons organic, unsalted butter or ghee
1 cup blueberries, and extra for optional garnish
½ cup pure maple syrup

Pancakes:
3 cups grated sweet potatoes (approx. 1 large)
⅓ cup walnut meal
1 teaspoon gluten free baking powder
1 teaspoon baking soda
2 teaspoons ground cinnamon
Pinch of sea salt
¼ cup coconut flour
5 large eggs
¼ cup unsweetened applesauce

In a small saucepan, heat syrup ingredients, on medium. While heating, use a spoon and "smoosh" the blueberries, until all are broken down (approx. 5 minutes). Continue cooking and stirring, until desired consistency. Remove from heat. Set aside.

Combine dry pancake ingredients, set aside. In a second bowl, whisk eggs. Add applesauce to eggs and mix.
Fold wet ingredients into dry ingredients ~ do not over stir.

Melt butter on a griddle or large skillet over medium heat.
Drop ¼ cup of batter, per pancake, onto griddle.
Flip pancakes when edges start to look slightly dry.
Pancakes are done when slightly brown.

Plate pancakes. Drizzle with syrup. Top with fresh blueberries (optional).

Yield: 8 large pancakes

Enjoy!

Chocolate Dipped Doughnut Holes

Doughnuts:
5 large eggs
1 banana
¼ cup coconut flour
Pinch of sea salt
3 Medjool dates, pitted and
    finely chopped
¼ cup creamy almond butter
1 teaspoon pure vanilla extract
2 tablespoons cocoa powder
1 teaspoon instant coffee
    crystals
½ teaspoon gluten free
    baking powder

Optional Toppings:
5-6 ounces dark chocolate
    (72% or higher)
¼ cup crushed walnuts
¼ cup unsweetened coconut
    flakes

Preheat doughnut hole maker (or a doughnut hole pan can be used).

In a mixing bowl, combine eggs, banana, coconut flour, sea salt, dates, almond butter, vanilla, cocoa powder, coffee crystals, and baking powder, until blended.

Fill the bottom half of a doughnut hole or cake pop maker with mixture, until level. Close lid and cook for approximately 3 minutes, until firm and slightly browned. Repeat, with remaining batter. Cool on a wire cooling rack.

While the doughnut holes are cooling, heat chocolate in a double boiler on low, until melted.

After doughnut holes have cooled for approximately 20 minutes, dip the tops of the doughnuts in the chocolate. (OPTIONAL STEPS: Dip chocolate-dipped doughnut holes into crushed walnuts or coconut flakes). Place back on the cooling rack. Repeat.

Yield: 30 doughnut holes

Enjoy!

Nutty Orangeberry Breakfast Muffins

5 large eggs

4 tablespoons organic, unsalted butter or ghee, softened

⅓ cup freshly squeezed orange juice

½ teaspoon pure vanilla extract

½ teaspoon orange extract

⅓ cup almond butter, creamy

1 tablespoon of fresh orange zest (approximately 1 large orange)

⅓ cup raw honey

⅓ cup coconut flour

1 teaspoon gluten free baking powder

⅓ cup crushed raw pecans

⅓ cup blueberries

Preheat oven to 350°F.

Grease 8 sections of a muffin tin.

Whisk eggs in a metal bowl until fluffy. Add butter, orange juice, vanilla, and orange extract. Blend.

Add almond butter, orange zest, and honey. Blend.

Add coconut flour and baking powder. Slowly combine until all ingredients are wet. Do not over blend.

Fold in pecans and blueberries.

Add batter to the muffin tin and bake for 25 minutes or until a toothpick can be inserted and removed dry.

Yield: 8 muffins

Enjoy!

Chocolate Waffles
with Raspberry Maple Syrup

Syrup:
½ cup pure maple syrup
½ cup fresh raspberries

Waffles:
⅓ cup unsweetened cocoa
1 teaspoon pure vanilla extract
6 large eggs
⅓ cup coconut flour
⅓ cup almond butter
¼ cup unsweetened apple-
   sauce
1 small banana
1 teaspoon gluten free
   baking powder
4 tablespoons organic,
   unsalted butter or ghee,
   softened
Pinch of sea salt

Cook syrup ingredients in a saucepan over medium heat, until raspberries are broken down. Cool. Strain through a sieve/strainer to remove seeds. Set aside.

Preheat waffle iron.

Mix waffle ingredients until blended. Pour necessary amount onto waffle iron and cook until done.

Plate waffles. Top with syrup.

Optional Toppings: fresh raspberries and walnuts

Yield: 2-3 Belgian waffles

Enjoy!

Maple Sage Breakfast Sausage

I received a meat grinder attachment for Christmas, and I finally got around to using it. I didn't realize how easy homemade sausage was to make! This recipe is for "bulk" sausage. You can use it in recipes, like my Breakfast Casserole, or form into patties.

1½ pounds pork butt, cubed

12 ounces applewood smoked bacon, nitrate-free

½ cup pure maple syrup

2 tablespoons sage, finely chopped

1 tablespoon finely chopped rosemary

1 teaspoon sea salt

¼ teaspoon ground celery seed

¼ teaspoon ground cinnamon

1 small apple, peeled, grated

Feed the pork butt cubes and bacon through your meat grinder. I alternate the meats. This combines them together nicely.

Add remaining ingredients to sausage mixture. Use your hands, or a spoon, and thoroughly blend all of the ingredients together.

For patties: Roll a golf ball-sized amount of sausage between the palms of your hands. Gently "smoosh" them down into a skillet, to form a patty. Cook for about 4 minutes per side, until center is done.

Enjoy!

Breakfast Casserole

1 pound Maple Sage Breakfast Sausage (page 23), or preferred sausage (bulk or cut from casings)
1 parsnip, peeled and grated
1 large sweet potato, peeled and grated
1 cup fresh spinach
1 onion, chopped
2 tablespoons organic, unsalted butter or ghee
1 tablespoon arrowroot
8 ounces organic heavy cream
6 large eggs

Preheat oven to 350°F.

Cook sausage until fully browned, in a medium skillet.

In a medium bowl, mix grated parsnip and sweet potato, until evenly distributed.
Layer your ingredients, in a greased 8 .5 x 11 baking dish:
Layer 1: Half of sweet potato mixture
Layer 2: All of spinach
Layer 3: All of sausage
Layer 4: Remaining sweet potato mixture

In same skillet, cook onion, until translucent. Add butter and arrowroot. Stir. Once butter is melted, add cream. Bring to boil.
Reduce heat and simmer for a couple of minutes, to slightly thicken.

Whisk eggs in medium bowl. Add 1-2 ladles of cream mixture to eggs to temper the eggs (so as to not create scrambled eggs). Pour egg mixture back into skillet and stir.
Pour skillet mixture over the top of the layers, in your baking dish.
Spread egg mixture to edges to form a seal when cooking.
Bake 30 minutes.
Remove from oven. Rest for approximately 30 minutes, allowing dish to set.

Enjoy!

2-Egg Omelette

2 pieces of bacon, small diced
1 shallot, peeled and diced
½ cup mushrooms, sliced or
   diced
¼ cup greens (I usually use
   spinach but I had some leftover mache that I used)
2 large eggs
¼ avocado, sliced
1 small Roma tomato, sliced
Sea salt and ground pepper,
   to taste

In a small skillet, place diced bacon and cook on medium heat, until almost crisp. Add shallots and mushrooms and continue to cook until tender. Add greens, with 30 seconds to go, so that they can wilt down. Using a slotted-spoon, transfer skillet ingredients to a small bowl. Set aside.

Whisk 2 eggs in bowl, until fluffy.

Reheat the skillet to medium-high. Pour in whisked eggs. Holding skillet about 2 inches above your burner, slowly swirl in a circular motion to continually distribute the eggs around the skillet. If you prefer a "chunkier" omelette, just take your spatula and create a few slashes in the cooked portion of the egg... the uncooked portion will fill in those gaps.

Once the egg is cooked, to your desired doneness (I like mine where the egg is just about set), transfer the bacon and veggie mixture to one half of the omelette. Take your spatula and flip the plain side over the filled side. Transfer to a plate.

Garnish with tomatoes and avocado. Salt and pepper, to taste.

Enjoy!

Reuben Benedict

½ pound corned beef
or pastrami
2 large eggs
1½ cups sauerkraut

Dijon Hollandaise Sauce:
2 egg yolks, beaten
2 teaspoons water
2 teaspoons freshly squeezed
lemon juice
½ teaspoon Sriracha
(or preferred hot sauce)
1 tablespoon Dijon mustard
¼ cup + 1 tablespoon organic,
unsalted butter or ghee

Caraway seeds (for garnish)

Place corned beef in a skillet and cook on low, until warm. Meanwhile, poach your eggs.

Divide corned beef into two portions and plate each. Top each with ½ cup of sauerkraut. Next, place a poached egg on each pile of sauerkraut.

For hollandaise sauce: Place ingredients in the top part of a double boiler (don't let the boiling water below touch the top pan). Slowly add pieces of butter. Whisk slowly and continuously, until butter melts and sauce thickens.

Pour hollandaise over each stack. Garnish with caraway seeds, as desired.

Serves 2

Enjoy!

Cavegirl Tip Fermented foods, such as sauerkraut, are a crucial part of the Paleo lifestyle. They are essential to keeping our digestive and immune systems strong.

Eggstraordinary Lox Benedict

4 ounces wild smoked salmon
(the fresher, the better!)
2 poached eggs
2 cups spinach
2 tablespoons capers
2 slices of red onion
2 thick tomato slices
4 tablespoons hollandaise
sauce (recipe below)
Sea salt and ground pepper,
to taste

Hollandaise Sauce:
¼ cup + 1 tablespoon ghee or
unsalted organic butter
2 beaten egg yolks
2 teaspoons water
2 teaspoons freshly squeezed
lemon juice
Dash of cayenne pepper

**Place greens in a lidded skillet with 1 tablespoon water.
Let steam 2-3 minutes until wilted. Meanwhile, poach your eggs.**

**To make the hollandaise, place ingredients in the top part of
a double boiler (don't let the boiling water below touch the
top pan), slowly adding the butter. Stir continuously until the
butter melts and the sauce thickens. Enjoy any extra sauce over
asparagus or fish (or both for a great dinner!).**

**Place a slice of tomato on the plate. Top the tomato with half
of the wilted greens. Place red onion on the greens.
Next is 2 ounces of the salmon and then a poached egg.
Pour 2 tablespoons hollandaise over the stack. Garnish with
1 tablespoon capers, salt and pepper.**

Serves 2

Enjoy!

Paleo Honey Crunches Cereal

1 cup unsalted sunflower seeds
1 cup unsweetened coconut
    flakes
1 cup unsalted walnut pieces
¼ cup dried unsweetened
    cherries, chopped
2 tablespoons raw almond
    butter
¼ cup raw honey
¼ cup coconut flour
Organic, virgin coconut oil,
    (enough to grease pan)

Preheat oven to 350˚F.

Place ingredients in a bowl and mix until well blended. Press mixture evenly onto a greased 9x13 pan.

Bake 15-20 minutes, until browned. Cool 30 minutes.

Crumble into an airtight container, for storage.

To serve: Pour unsweetened coconut milk over the cereal. Feel free to use whatever "milk" fits with your dietary needs or taste preferences.

Yield: approximately 3 cups

Enjoy!

Variations: (1) Add fresh blueberries or other fruit (2) Without milk, this is also great for a car snack or a pick-me-up, during a weekend hike, as a granola substitute!

 To grease a pan with coconut oil, slightly melt the oil and then use a pastry brush to coat the pan.

Choco-Hazelnut Paleo Cereal

1 cup unsalted sunflower seeds

1 cup unsweetened coconut flakes

1 cup unsalted hazelnuts, roughly chopped

⅓ cup unsweetened cocoa powder

¼ cup dried unsweetened cherries, chopped

2 tablespoons raw almond butter

¼ cup pure maple syrup

¼ cup coconut flour

Organic, virgin coconut oil, (enough to grease pan)

Preheat oven to 350°F.

Place ingredients in a bowl and mix until well blended. Press mixture evenly into a greased 9x13 pan.

Bake for 15-20 minutes, until browned. Cool for 30 minutes.

Crumble into an airtight container for storage.

To serve: Pour unsweetened coconut milk over the cereal. Feel free to use whatever "milk" fits with your dietary needs or taste preferences.

Yield: approximately 3 cups

Enjoy!

Noatmeal

1 cup raw unsalted sunflower
  seeds
1 cup unsweetened coconut
  flakes
1 cup unsalted pecan pieces
2 tablespoons almond butter,
  creamy
¼ cup raw honey
¼ cup coconut flour
Pinch of sea salt
Coconut oil, organic, virgin
  (enough to grease the pan)
⅓ cup coconut milk
  (or preferred milk)

Preheat oven to 350˚F.

Mix sunflower seeds, coconut, pecans, almond butter, honey, coconut flour, and salt until blended. Press mixture evenly into pan. Bake for 15-20 minutes, until browned on top. Cool for 30 minutes.

Transfer to a food processor or blender. Pulse several times, until broken down a bit, but still chunky.

In a small saucepan, bring ⅓-cup coconut milk to a rolling boil. Add ½ cup of noatmeal to the saucepan. Stir and remove from heat. Transfer to a serving bowl and add additional coconut milk, if desired.

Store remaining noatmeal in a sealed container for up to 7 days.

Yield: 3½ cups

Enjoy!

By Land

By Land

1 whole free-range chicken
Extra virgin olive oil
2 teaspoons avocado oil
1-2 teaspoons sea salt and
    ground pepper
1-2 tablespoons of Italian
    seasoning
1 lemon or lime
1 orange or apple
½ cup water
3-4 roughly chopped garlic
    cloves
½ roughly chopped onion
¼ cup water

For broth:
2 stalks chopped celery
1-2 chopped carrots
1-2 teaspoons sea salt and
    ground pepper
6 cups water

Preheat oven to 350°F.

Remove any chicken innards. Give your bird an avocado oil massage (inside and out) with about 2 tablespoons of the oil. Season liberally, with salt, pepper, and preferred seasonings/rub.

Stab your lemon/lime and your apple/orange several times with a knife. Insert both into the chicken cavity.

Place chicken into a covered Dutch oven (or other preferred roasting pan). Pour in water. Add garlic and onion to the pan. Cook for 1½ to 2 hours, or until thoroughly cooked (175°F when a thermometer is inserted into the breast). However, cook uncovered for the last 30 minutes. Let rest for 20-30 minutes. Pull chicken apart from the bones.

To make the chicken broth, place the chicken carcass in a crock-pot. Pour 6 cups of water over the bones. Include some of the Dutch oven ingredients (onions and the garlic cloves). Add 2 stalks of chopped celery. Add 1-2 chopped carrots. Add 1-2 teaspoons sea salt. Add any veggie scraps you have in your refrigerator. Cook on low overnight. Strain ingredients.

Yield: 6 cups of flavorful, fresh chicken broth for your soup of choice!

Enjoy!

Chicken Sausage & Kale Portabellas

4 large portabella mushrooms
1 teaspoon bacon grease
or ghee
½ pound Italian chicken
sausage, bulk or casings
removed
½ seeded bell pepper, diced
1 cup finely chopped kale
¼ teaspoon sea salt
2-3 garlic cloves, peeled and
minced
1 tablespoon avocado oil (or
preferred oil)

Preheat oven to 350°F.

Clean mushrooms and remove stems. Finely dice the mushroom stems and set mushroom caps aside.

Heat bacon grease in a skillet, over medium heat.
Add mushroom stems, sausage, peppers, kale and salt. Cook until sausage is almost done. Add garlic and toss. Remove from heat.

Mist or brush avocado oil onto the mushroom caps, in a baking pan. Stuff each mushroom with sausage mixture. Pour about 1 tablespoon of water into the bottom of the baking pan. Cover pan with an aluminum foil tent (This will steam the mushrooms while baking).

Bake 15 minutes. Remove foil. Resume baking, uncovered, for an additional 10 minutes. Cool for about 10 minutes. Tip mushrooms before plating to discard any excess liquid.

Yield: 4 stuffed mushrooms

Enjoy!

Paleo Chicken Lettuce Wraps

My mom and I love to go to a certain "China Bistro" for lunch, as I can usually order simple salmon and broccoli for my meal. Occasionally, as a "cheat", we'll get a glass of chardonnay and split the chicken lettuce wraps ~ it's such a treat! Below is my version!

1 tablespoon sesame oil
1 pound ground chicken
5 ounces shiitake mushrooms, finely diced
⅓ cup scallions, chopped
1 tablespoon fresh ginger, peeled, minced
3 tablespoons coconut aminos
4-5 cloves of garlic, peeled and minced
¼ cup slivered almonds
1 tablespoon white wine vinegar
1 teaspoon Dijon mustard
1 tablespoon Sriracha (or preferred hot sauce)
1 tablespoon raw honey
¼ teaspoon sea salt
16 Boston lettuce leaves

In a skillet, heat sesame oil on medium heat. Add ground chicken. Cook until almost done.

Add mushrooms, scallions, ginger, and coconut aminos. Cook until scallions and mushrooms are translucent. Stir in garlic, almonds, white wine vinegar, Dijon mustard, Sriracha, honey, and salt. Remove from heat.

Place lettuce cups on a plate. Serve the chicken mixture in a bowl and let your guests spoon the mixture onto the center of the leaves. Hold like a soft taco to eat.

Garnish with chopped scallions if desired.

Serves 4

Enjoy!

Tangerine Chicken

¼ cup coconut aminos

1 tablespoon tangerine zest strips (the outer rind), cut into half matchsticks

1 teaspoon tangerine zest

2 tablespoons fresh tangerine juice

1 tablespoon cooking Sherry

1½ pounds chicken thighs, cut into strips

2 teaspoons + 1 tablespoon sesame oil

1 red pepper, julienned

3 scallions, chopped, separate white and green parts

1 tablespoon fresh ginger, peeled, minced

1 tablespoon fresh tangerine juice

¼ cup raw honey

1 tablespoon arrowroot

2 tablespoons toasted sesame seeds, for garnish

Combine coconut aminos, tangerine zest strips, tangerine zest, tangerine juice, cooking Sherry, and 2 teaspoons sesame oil. Add chicken strips. Cover and marinate in refrigerator for a minimum of 30 minutes. Remove chicken. Discard marinade.

In a wok or skillet, heat 1 tablespoon sesame oil on medium heat. Add red pepper and the chopped white part of the scallions. Cook on medium heat until tender (approximately 2-3 minutes).

Add ginger, 1 tablespoon of tangerine juice, honey, arrowroot, and marinated chicken. Cover and cook for 5 minutes, on medium heat. Remove lid and continue to cook until sauce thickens and chicken is cooked through. Add about ¼ cup of the green part of the chopped scallions.

Remove from heat. Garnish with toasted sesame seeds.

Serves 2

Enjoy!

 If you don't have access to tangerines, substitute oranges or mandarins.

Stuffed Chicken Breast

This recipe is easy to make and the results are beautiful (and tasty). I have made this hundreds of times, but never the same way twice. Use what you have in the refrigerator… change the flavor profile with spices… have fun!

2 chicken boneless breasts
Sea salt and ground pepper, to taste
Approximately 10 fresh basil leaves
2 slices of prosciutto (nitrate-free)
½ roasted red pepper, cut in half
¼ teaspoon dried lemongrass
1 large egg
2 teaspoons of yellow mustard
½ cup coarsely ground almond meal

Preheat oven to 350°F.

Place chicken breasts between two pieces of parchment paper. Using the flat side of a meat mallet, bang the chicken until it is about ¼–inch thick.

Remove top layer of parchment paper. Season top of chicken breast with salt and pepper. Layer basil on top of the chicken. Next, add one slice of prosciutto onto each breast. Layer the roasted red pepper. Season with ground lemongrass.

Carefully roll up each chicken breast starting with the narrower end and rolling towards the wider end.

Whisk the egg and yellow mustard in a small bowl. Place the almond meal in a separate bowl. Using a pastry brush, coat a roll with the egg wash and then with the almond meal. Do this with both chicken breasts.

Place the chicken rolls, seam side down, in a lightly greased baking dish. Cook for 25-30 minutes, until the chicken is thoroughly cooked. Rest for approximately 10 minutes.

Enjoy!

Teriyaki Chicken Thighs

⅓ cup coconut aminos
¼ cup pure maple syrup
¼ cup apple cider vinegar
1 tablespoon sesame oil
1 tablespoon cooking Sherry
½ teaspoon crushed red
    pepper flakes
2 teaspoon fresh ginger,
    peeled, grated
5 cloves of garlic, peeled,
    minced
4 pounds of chicken thighs
    (about 5 thighs)
2 tablespoons toasted sesame
    seeds

Preheat oven to 350˚F.

Combine coconut aminos, maple syrup, apple cider vinegar, sesame oil, cooking Sherry, red pepper flakes, ginger, and garlic, creating a marinade.

Place chicken, packed tightly, in a small dish. Pour marinade over the chicken. Cover and refrigerate for approximately an hour. Flip chicken and let marinate for another hour.

Transfer chicken to a baking dish. Set aside excess marinade. Spoon a teaspoon of the marinade over each thigh. Bake 15 minutes. Flip chicken. Add additional marinade, if necessary, and continue to cook until desired doneness, approximately 15 minutes.

Plate chicken and sprinkle with toasted sesame seeds.

Serves 4

Enjoy!

Spicy Grilled Chicken Tenders

7 chicken tenders
1 tablespoon Sriracha
   (or preferred hot sauce)
1 tablespoon yellow mustard
1 teaspoon raw honey or
   pure maple syrup
Chopped cilantro (or parsley or
   basil)

Mix hot sauce, mustard, and honey.

Skewer chicken tenders. Brush sauce over the chicken.

Cook chicken on a greased grill or a grill pan for 3-4 minutes per side until cooked.

Garnish with cilantro.

Yield: 7 chicken tenders

Enjoy!

Turkey Bacon Sliders

1 pound ground turkey
6 slices nitrate-free bacon,
    finely chopped
½ sweet onion, finely diced
½ teaspoon sea salt
1 teaspoon garlic powder

Mix all ingredients in a bowl. Form into large golf balls. Flatten and smooth into patties. Set aside.

Grease your grill or grilling pan and heat to medium-high.

Cook patties for 4-5 minutes per side or until internal temperature reaches at least 160°F.

Remove from heat source and let rest for about 5 minutes.

Yield: 4 sliders

Enjoy!

Cranberry-Glazed Quail with Jalapeño-Bacon Brussels Sprouts

Glaze:
1 cup fresh cranberries
1 Granny Smith apple (or tart apple), grated
¼ cup pure maple syrup
1 teaspoon cooking Sherry
1 teaspoon grated nutmeg
½ teaspoon cinnamon
2 tablespoons freshly squeezed orange juice
⅓ cup water

Brussels Sprouts:
4 cups quartered fresh Brussels sprouts
4 slices of bacon, diced (I took my kitchen shears and cut it down randomly)
1 large jalapeno, seeded and diced

Quail:
4 quail (about a pound total)
1 small lemon, quartered
several sprigs of thyme
4 small pats of ghee or unsalted organic butter
Sea salt and ground pepper, to taste

Make the glaze (this can be done the night before). In a medium saucepan, place all of the glaze ingredients and cook over medium heat. Stir. The cranberries will start to pop and break down. Continue to stir while smooshing the cranberries against the side of the pan. Do this for about 10 minutes. Let cool. Press mixture through a sieve or fine mesh strainer. Discard solid ingredients left in the mesh. Refrigerate liquid.

Preheat oven to 350˚F. In a baking pan, place Brussels sprouts, bacon, and jalapeno. Cook on the top rack for 40 minutes, stirring mixture every 10 minutes to distribute the bacon fat as it cooks.

In the meantime, rinse quail and pat dry with a paper towel. Stuff each quail with a lemon, 1-2 sprigs of thyme, and a pat of butter. Season with salt and pepper. Tie legs together (if you have baker's twine… if not, don't worry about it). Place in an 8×8 baking dish. Brush ⅓ of the glaze on the birds. Pour 2-3 tablespoons of water in the bottom of the pan. Cover dish like a tent with a piece of aluminum foil. Place on the bottom rack of the oven and cook for 15 minutes. Brush another ⅓ of the glaze on. Cover and cook for an additional 10 minutes. Remove foil. Place under the broiler for about 6-7 minutes to brown. The internal temperature of the birds should be at least 160˚F (to me, the meat thermometer is one of my essential tools).

Remove from oven. Let rest for 10 minutes.

Garnish with additional thyme if desired. Serve immediately.

Enjoy!

Pork Tenderloin with Sweet Cherry Sauce

The sweetness of the cherries, with the saltiness and smokiness of the pork, marries these flavors beautifully in this delish dish!

1 tablespoon walnut oil
(or preferred oil)
1-2 pork tenderloin(s)
Sea salt and ground pepper
2 cups fresh, sweet cherries,
pitted
2 teaspoons red wine vinegar
2 tablespoons water
2 tablespoons broth
1 tablespoon raw honey
½ teaspoon ground cinnamon

Preheat oven to 350°F.

Heat a skillet on medium-high heat, with 1 tablespoon walnut oil. Season pork tenderloin(s) liberally with salt and pepper. Sear approximately 1 minute per side.

In a lightly greased baking dish, bake tenderloin(s), until desired doneness (approximately 30 minutes, depending on the size of the loin). I prefer an internal temperature of 160-165°F.

While tenderloin is baking, place remaining ingredients in the sear pan and heat on medium heat, scraping the bits into the sauce. Taking a fork or the side of your mixing spoon, "smoosh" the cherries. Bring the heat up and let the mixture come to a boil, while continuing to smoosh the cherries. Simmer. Allow to thicken for about 5-7 minutes. If the sauce gets too thick, just add a little water (a tablespoon at a time, until desired consistency).

Remove tenderloin from oven. Rest 10 minutes. Slice. Serve with cherry sauce over the pork.

Serves 4-6

Enjoy!

Fall Off the Bone Ribs

1 rack of pork ribs
2 teaspoons sea salt
1 teaspoon smoked paprika
1 teaspoon cracked black
    pepper
½ teaspoon cayenne pepper
2 teaspoons garlic powder
2 tablespoons avocado oil
    (or preferred oil)
2 tablespoons water
½ onion, roughly chopped

Preheat oven to 250˚F.

Combine salt, paprika, black pepper, cayenne pepper, and garlic powder.

Place ribs in a large baking dish. Brush oil over the top and bottom of ribs. Sprinkle the rub liberally over the entire rack.

Scatter the chopped onions around the baking dish. Add water.

Using aluminum foil, create a "tent" over the dish, sealing the foil around the edges of the dish.

Cook for 3 hours on the bottom oven rack. Remove foil and baste the ribs with the juices. Continue to cook uncovered on the top oven rack for an additional 45 minutes, basting about every 15 minutes.

Let ribs rest for about 10 minutes. Cut between bones and serve.

Serves 2-3

Enjoy!

BBQ Pulled Pork Wraps (Slow Cooker)

1 head of Bibb lettuce

Slow Cooker Ingredients:
2 pound bone-in pork butt
(or pork shoulder roast)
½ large red onion, roughly
chopped
4-6 garlic cloves, peeled and
quartered
2 cups chicken or beef broth
2 cups water
Sea salt and ground pepper,
to taste

BBQ Sauce:
½ cup marinara sauce
⅛ cup pure maple syrup
1 tablespoon Sriracha
(or preferred hot sauce)
1 teaspoon Worcestershire
sauce

Place slow cooker ingredients in a slow cooker on low heat.
If the liquid does not cover the pork, then add enough to do so.
Cook for 6 hours on low, turning once or twice during cooking time.
If possible, occasionally spoon any liquid back over the exposed
portion of the meat.

In the meantime, mix the BBQ sauce ingredients together.
Transfer to a lidded container and refrigerate, until ready to use.

Note: I prefer to make the sauce the night before to let the flavors really
come together, but immediate use is still very good!

Once the pork is cooked and tender, transfer to a cutting board. Cool
15 minutes. Using a pair of forks, start "pulling" the pork apart into strips.
Discard bone.

Transfer meat to large bowl and mix in BBQ sauce.

Spoon mixture into washed lettuce leaves. Eat taco-style. You may also
want to scoop the onions out of the slow cooker and add to your wraps as
a bonus!

Enjoy!

 If you are serving children or adults who don't like spice,
reduce the amount of Sriracha added to the BBQ sauce
and then just add extra to your serving for an additional kick!

French Cut Pork Chops
with Brussels Sprouts & Apple Slaw

1 pound Brussels sprouts,
 roughly chopped
1 tablespoon bacon grease
2 teaspoons fresh lemon juice
2 Granny Smith apples
3 French cut, bone-in pork
 chops (about 1½ pounds)
3 tablespoons Dijon mustard
Sea salt and ground pepper,
 to taste
1 tablespoon extra virgin olive oil

Preheat oven to 350°F.

**In a baking dish, mix the chopped Brussels sprouts with
the bacon grease. Bake for 30 minutes. Set aside to cool.**

**Put the lemon juice in a medium bowl. Grate apples down to the
core, into the lemon juice. Stir occasionally, to prevent the apples
from browning. Add Brussels sprouts and olive oil. Stir ingredients
to coat evenly.**

**Season the pork chops with salt and pepper, on both sides.
Place on heated grill (I used a grill pan, on the stovetop).
Cook until desired doneness (I like mine at 160°F ~ medium).
Rest 5 minutes.**

**Plate one tablespoon of mustard on a plate. Put a third of the slaw
in a pile on the plate. Lean a pork chop against the slaw.**

Yield: 3 pork chops

Enjoy!

Gyro Salad

2½ pounds lamb shoulder

1 small onion, roughly chopped

1 head Romaine lettuce,
    cleaned and chopped

Marinade:

¼ cup avocado oil
    (or preferred oil)

1 teaspoon smoked paprika

1 tablespoon fresh oregano
    leaves, chopped

½ teaspoon garlic salt

2 teaspoons ground coriander

½ teaspoon chili powder

¼ teaspoon ground cinnamon

Tomato and Onion Salad:

¾ cup tomatoes, seeded and diced

½ red onion, sliced

¼ cup extra virgin olive oil

½ cup apple cider vinegar

¼ cup water

Dash of preferred hot sauce

Sea salt and ground pepper, to taste

Tzatziki Sauce:

1 cucumber, peeled, seeded and diced

½ cup heavy whipping cream,

Organic juice of 1 lime

2-3 cloves of garlic, minced

1 teaspoon sea salt (more, for taste, if necessary)

2 tablespoons fresh dill, chopped

Stir marinade ingredients. Pour over lamb. Refrigerate, covered, for 1 hour.

Preheat oven to 250°F.

Place lamb into a Dutch oven or heavy pot. Place roughly chopped onion around the meat, in the pot. Cover.
Cook 1½ hours.

While cooking, place all of the tomato and onion salad ingredients in a bowl. Stir. Refrigerate.

For the Tzatziki sauce: Beat ¼ cup of the whipping cream, until firm peaks form. Add remaining ingredients (including remaining cream) stirring on low until blended. Taste. Add salt, as necessary. The consistency should be that of a dressing. Refrigerate.

Let lamb rest for 10-15 minutes, after removing from the oven. Thinly slice for plating.

Use chopped romaine as a base on the plate. Add meat.
Using a slotted spoon, add tomato and onion salad. Spoon some of the Tzatziki sauce on top.

Optional Toppings: Freshly ground pepper and chopped dill.

Enjoy!

If dairy is not a concern of yours, you can double the Tzatziki Sauce. The amount made here is minimal, as to just give the flavor of a traditional Tzatziki Sauce, for my die-hards!

Lamb Kebab with Mint Pesto

Mint Pesto:

1 cup fresh mint leaves
1 cup fresh parsley
¼ medium onion
⅓ cup pine nuts
2 garlic cloves
5 tablespoons extra virgin olive oil
1 teaspoon lemon zest
1 teaspoon sea salt

Lamb Kebabs:

1 pound ground lamb
1 cup chopped parsley
1 large egg
Juice from ½ of a lemon
¼ medium onion, minced
1 tablespoon raw honey
½ teaspoon ground black
    pepper
½ teaspoon ground coriander
½ teaspoon paprika
½ teaspoon ground celery seed
8 skewers

In a food processor, combine all of the mint pesto ingredients. Blend until smooth. Refrigerate.

In a large bowl, combine all ingredients for the kebabs and toss, until evenly mixed. Divide the mixture into eight servings. Form each serving around a skewer, creating four sides. Grill (about 2 minutes per side).

Yield: 8 kebabs

Enjoy!

 If you choose to grow your own mint, I would recommend using a planter instead of growing it freely. When I moved into my home a few years back, the previous owner planted mint and it was everywhere! Each summer, I spend a lot of my time thinning and pulling up rogue mint leaves!

Lamb Loin Chops (simple & family-style)

Marinade:
1 tablespoon red wine vinegar
Juice of one lemon
1 teaspoon sea salt
¼ cup avocado oil
1-2 sprigs rosemary

1½ pounds lamb loin chops (5-6)
1 tablespoon ghee or organic
    unsalted butter
2 cups organic diced tomatoes
    (including juice)
8 ounces button mushrooms,
    quartered
2-3 cloves of garlic, minced
3 fresh sage leaves,
    finely chopped
Sea salt and ground pepper,
    to taste
1 tablespoon fresh thyme leaves

In a gallon plastic storage bag, combine marinade ingredients. Add lamb, while removing as much air as possible. Refrigerate 30 minutes.

In a large skillet, melt butter on medium-high heat. Add lamb loin chops (discard marinade).

Cook both sides of lamb evenly until desired doneness (I took mine up to 135°F internal temperature. The USDA recommendation is 150°F). Set aside to rest.

In the same pan, add tomatoes and mushrooms, scraping brown bits of the pan to add to the flavor. Cook on medium heat for approximately 3 minutes. Add garlic, sage, salt, and pepper. Bring to boil. Turn down heat and simmer for approximately 5 minutes.

Add tomato mixture to a serving bowl. Arrange chops on top. Garnish with fresh thyme.

Serves 3-4

Enjoy!

Tenderloin & Arugula Salad

Vinaigrette:
6 tablespoons extra virgin
   olive oil
2 tablespoons balsamic
   vinegar
3 teaspoons horseradish
Pinch of sea salt

Beef:
1 pound beef tenderloin
Sea salt and ground pepper,
   to taste

Arugula Salad:
4 cups arugula
20 pecan halves
16 cherry tomatoes, halved
1 cup blueberries
¼ cup edible flowers
½ cup pomegranate seeds

Whisk vinaigrette ingredients. Cover. Refrigerate.

Season beef, on both sides, with salt and pepper. Cook on stovetop or grill, until desired doneness. Remove from heat. Allow to rest for five minutes.

Divide salad ingredients among four plates. Thinly slice beef and divide among the four salads.

Drizzle vinaigrette over salads. Grind fresh pepper, as an optional garnish.

Serves 4

Enjoy!

Marinade:

2 tablespoon coconut aminos

1 tablespoon freshly grated
   ginger

¼ cup chopped onion

2 garlic cloves, peeled,
   quartered

1 tablespoon avocado oil

1 teaspoon Sriracha
   (or preferred hot sauce)

1 beef tenderloin
   (about 2-3 pounds)

Jar of store-bought kimchi

Toasted sesame seeds
   (optional garnish)

Place all ingredients in a lidded container or disposable plastic bag, with the beef. Marinate in the refrigerator for an hour.

Grill to desired doneness. Thinly slice the meat, against the grain. Serve with kimchi. Garnish with sesame seeds (optional).

Serves 4

Enjoy!

BBQ Stud Muffins

I was watching TV one day and someone used the term "stud muffin". It made me think of on-the-go meatloaves. I knew that horses could be studs, but I had to look up the term, as horsemeat is hard to come by! Apparently, a stud is a breeder animal. There are such things as "stud cattle". Making beef my meat of choice! These BBQ Stud Muffins are great for a quick fix or served with broccoli and a sweet potato, for a complete meal!

BBQ Sauce:
½ cup marinara sauce (no sugar added)
¼ cup pure maple syrup
1 teaspoon Worcestershire sauce
1 teaspoon Dijon mustard

Muffins:
1 pound ground beef (85/15 mix)
1 large egg
½ cup almond meal
1 carrot, peeled and grated
2 green onions (green part included), minced
1 teaspoon sea salt
¼ teaspoon garlic powder
¼ teaspoon dried lemongrass
¼ teaspoon chili powder

Preheat oven to 350˚F.

In a small bowl, mix together BBQ sauce ingredients. Set aside.

In a large bowl, mix the remaining ingredients (use your hands. It's my preferred method). Add ½ cup of the BBQ Sauce. Reserve the remaining sauce.

Grease a muffin pan. I have a 6-muffin pan that makes larger than average muffins.

Fill the pan with the meat mixture. Glaze the tops of the muffins with the remaining sauce.

Cook for approximately 25 minutes (this will vary depending on the size of the muffins). For best results, use a meat thermometer for desired doneness.

Yield: 6-8 muffins

Enjoy!

 Use bacon grease to grease the muffin pan. It adds another level of flavor.

Ultimate Meatballs

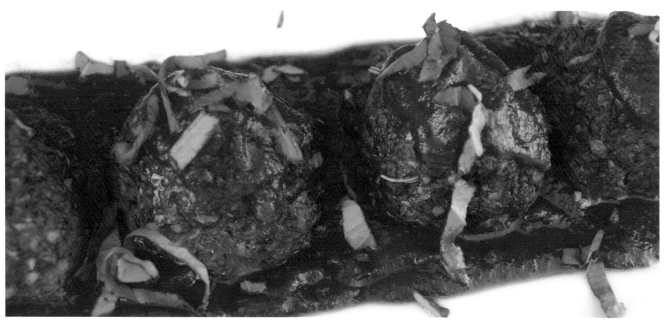

I love meatballs! I like them with my favorite marinara sauce, on spaghetti squash or even just heated up for a quick on-the-go snack. My version is chock full of protein and veggies.

4 ounces Baby Bella/crimini mushrooms, halved

1 stalk of celery, roughly chopped

1 carrot, peeled

Bunch of scallions, the bottom third (onion portion and a section of the greens)

1 pound ground beef

2 large eggs

⅓ cup almond meal

1 tablespoon dried parsley

1 teaspoon sea salt

¼ teaspoon cayenne pepper

¼ teaspoon ground cinnamon

1½ cups marinara (heated and reserved for plating)

Optional Garnish: fresh basil leaves

Preheat oven to 350°F.

In food processor, blend mushrooms, celery, carrots and scallions, until finely chopped.

In a bowl, add ground beef, ingredients from the food processor, eggs, almond meal, parsley, salt, cayenne pepper, and cinnamon. Thoroughly mix ingredients with your hands or a spoon.

Using an ice-cream scooper, scoop a ball of meat mixture (12 meatballs total) and place each one on a large, greased baking pan.

Cook for 35-40 minutes until preferred doneness. Remove and plate meatballs.

Spoon heated marinara sauce over meatballs. Garnish with chopped fresh basil. Serve.

Yield: 12 meatballs

Enjoy!

If you don't have time to make your own marinara, use a pre-made version. Just make sure to read the label and try to avoid those with hidden sugars and preservatives.

Endive Tacos

Belgian endive... enough to make about 30 boats

Salsa:
½ avocado, chopped into small cubes
2 garlic cloves, peeled, minced
1 large Roma tomato, chopped into small cubes
¼ red onion, finely chopped
2 tablespoons cilantro, plus extra for garnish
Juice of 1 lime
¼ teaspoon sea salt

Beef Mixture:
½ pound ground beef
⅓ cup Enchilada Sauce (page 115)

Mix salsa ingredients together. Refrigerate.

Cook meat on medium-high heat, until completely browned. Drain excess grease. Pour the enchilada sauce in the pan and cook 5 minutes, until a thick mixture is achieved.

Place a small amount of the meat mixture in an endive boat. Place an equal amount of salsa. Garnish with cilantro, if desired.

Yield: approximately 30 boats

Enjoy!

 These ingredients would be wonderful as a taco salad. Just roughly chop the endive (or preferred greens) and spoon beef mixture and salsa over the top of your salad.

Salsa Verde Meatballs

These are amazingly moist and delicious.

1 pound ground beef
¼ cup almond meal
1 large egg
½ cup onion, finely chopped
¼ cup Salsa Verde, plus ¼ cup
   per plate (page 116)
1 tablespoon fresh cilantro,
   chopped (plus extra for
   optional garnish)
¼ teaspoon smoked paprika
⅛ teaspoon red pepper flakes
½ teaspoon sea salt
½ teaspoon ground pepper

Thoroughly combine all ingredients. Form into golf ball sized balls (approximately 12). Place onto greased baking pan (I used bacon grease for added flavor). Bake, uncovered, 30 minutes.

Drizzle Salsa Verde on plate before adding your meatballs. Garnish with optional chopped fresh cilantro.

Yield: 12 meatballs

Enjoy!

Spiraled Rutabaga Bolognese

Another creation made with my vegetable spiral slicer… This is a kitchen gadget worth buying!

1 pound ground beef
1 small onion, diced
½ cup button mushrooms, chopped
2-4 cloves of garlic, peeled, minced
1½ cups of your favorite marinara
1 large rutabaga, peeled
Sea salt and ground pepper, to taste
Black truffle oil (or preferred oil)
Fresh Italian parsley, optional

In a pan, sauté beef, onion, mushrooms, and garlic, until ground beef is fully browned. Add marinara sauce. Bring to a boil. Reduce heat and simmer for 15 minutes.

Bring a pot of salted water to a boil (just as you would for pasta).

Cut off ends of the rutabaga. Using a vegetable spiraler, spiral rutabaga into spaghetti strands. Boil for 5 minutes, until tender.

Drain "rutabaga noodles" and plate. Drizzle oil over the noodles. For me, this is the most important step (drizzling oil over any vegetable noodle gives them a great flavor). Season lightly with salt.

Spoon sauce over noodles. Garnish with parsley. Serve.

Serves 4-6

Enjoy!

 If you don't own a vegetable spiraler, simply julienne the rutabaga instead.

This is just a back-to-basics easy Paleo meal ~ cheap, easy, and good!

1 pound ground beef
4 cups of mushrooms
    (I used a mixture of Baby
    Bellas and buttons),
    quartered
1 Vidalia onion, roughly
    chopped
1 tablespoon almond oil
Seasonings for burgers: Use whatever your favorite spices are!

Separate ground beef into quarters and form patties. Season liberally on both sides.

Heat oil in a skillet, over medium heat. Add mushrooms and onions. Cook until tender.

In the meantime, grill, until desired doneness. Rest 5 minutes.

Plate your patties and veggies. I added a few arugula leaves for color.

Yield: 4 burgers

Enjoy!

The Burger Solution

You can have your burger and eat it, too! However, avoid the "fast-food", pink slime, variety. Knowing where your burger comes from, and forgoing the bun and fries will keep you on track. Burgers are also very portable meals, for the lunch-packers out there. Instead of the typical burger sides, add a "rainbow" to your plate.

Ground beef (1 pound for
   4 quarter-pound burgers)
Ground pepper
Garlic salt
1 red onion
1 green pepper
Bacon grease
Dijon mustard (optional)
1 thick tomato slice
1 pint blueberries
2 tablespoons sliced nuts
   (any variety)

Season ground beef with ground pepper and garlic salt. Grill burgers to your liking. Then, let them rest for at least 3-5 minutes. To add wonderful flavor, serve with red onions and green peppers that were sautéed in a bit of bacon grease (natural fat), and a thick slice of tomato. For even more flavor, add a dollop of whole grain Dijon mustard.

On the side: Serve blueberries sprinkled with almond slices. Any berries or nuts will do. Just look around your kitchen and "fill" your plate with healthy options.

Enjoy!

 Don't use the back of your spatula to "smoosh" the burger, while grilling. Doing so will cause all of those wonderful juices to be lost.

Beef, Bacon & Caramelized Onion Bites

Here, meatloaf meets the smokiness of bacon and the sweetness of caramelized onions. I made this into appetizer bites, but you can use a regular-sized muffin pan for lunch or dinner portions.

1 pound ground beef

1 onion, finely chopped

2 slices of applewood smoked bacon, diced

¾ cup portabella mushrooms, diced

1 large egg

1 tablespoon Dijon mustard

½ cup pecan meal (pecans ground up in a food processor)

2 tablespoons salsa

Preheat oven to 350°F.

In a medium skillet, sauté onions and bacon on low for 35 minutes, stirring occasionally. Add mushrooms. Continue to sauté for an additional 10 minutes.

Combine beef, egg, mustard, pecan meal and salsa in a bowl, until well blended. Press meat mixture into mini muffin tin, pressing the meat on the bottom and up the sides (like a meat crust). Place in oven. Bake 7 minutes. Remove. Using a metal melon-baller (or the back of a spoon), press meat down again as it has a tendency to puff up. Resume baking for an additional 13 minutes.

Remove from the oven. Cool 5 minutes. Plate meat "crusts" and fill with mushroom/onion/bacon mixture. Serve.

Yield: 24 beef bites

Enjoy!

 Almond meal (or any preferred nut meal) can be substituted here for the pecan meal.

Seven Layer Mexican Dip

Perfect for football season! Chips and dip were always a part of my watching the Georgia Bulldogs. Over the years, I've had to adapt to fresher ways of eating and this dip is a way to bring in the new and celebrate the past... yummy flavors! Because there is the lack of the crunchy tortillas, I make the bacon layer extra crispy to compensate for that missed texture.

Layer 1: 1 pound cooked and seasoned, according to the packet, ground beef (any taco seasoning packet, which is non-GMO and without preservatives, is preferable).

Layer 2: 1½ cups green onions, chopped

Layer 3: 3 tomatoes, seeded and diced and seasoned with salt and pepper, to taste

Layer 4: 1 cup jarred nopalitos (tender cactus), drained and diced

Layer 5: 1½ cups guacamole

Layer 6: 5.75-ounce can of jumbo black olives, sliced

Layer 7: 1 pound bacon, cooked crispy and chopped

Optional Garnish: 1 bunch of chopped cilantro and juice of 1 lime

After layers have been "built", serve with large spoon.

Serve with Bibb lettuce. Spoon mixture into separate lettuce leaves, as you would with soft tacos.

Enjoy!

 If there is a layer that you don't like and don't want to use, just eliminate or substitute that ingredient. Rachael G. from California made this for her office potluck and substituted the nopalitos with chopped artichoke hearts ~ it was a hit!

2, 2-inch veal shanks
⅛ cup coconut flour
Sea salt and ground pepper
2 tablespoons unsalted,
    organic butter or ghee
1¼ cups mushrooms
    (your choice of variety ~
    I used bellas)
1 small yellow onion, chunked
1 large carrot, peeled
1 celery stalk
1 cup of dry white wine
1 cup beef stock

Gremolata:
2 tablespoons fresh parsley,
    chopped
Zest of 1 lemon
3 garlic cloves, peeled, minced

Preheat oven to 325°F.

Pat the shanks dry with a paper towel. Lightly dredge the shanks in coconut flour and liberally season with salt and pepper.

In a Dutch oven, melt butter, on medium-high heat. Add shanks and brown on all sides. Remove from pot. Set aside.

In food processor, place mushrooms, onion, carrot, and celery and pulse until finely chopped. Add to the pot that was used to brown the shanks. Cook until tender. Add white wine. Stir, scraping the "brown bits" from the bottom of the pan. Bring to a boil and reduce liquid by half. Add broth and stir.

Add shanks to the mixture. Cover. Place in oven and cook 2 hours.

While shanks are cooking, mix Gremolata ingredients and refrigerate.

After 2 hours, remove Dutch oven. Keep lid on, let rest for 15 minutes.

To serve, place a shank on a plate. Spoon veggie mixture around the shank. Sprinkle liberally with the Gremolata.

Enjoy!

 Don't be afraid to try different varieties of wine. A dry red wine would give a different, but equally yummy, flavor profile.

Cottage Pie

One of the most requested recipes is Shepherd's Pie. After much reading, I learned that Shepherd's Pie includes ground lamb and Cottage Pie generally includes beef. I found that mushrooms were "allowed" in both, as well. This recipe seems to have old roots... almost like a veggie soup... basically, whatever you have in the fridge/pantry, use. I used a variety of meats; however, use whatever ground meat you have on hand. Also use whatever veggies you have available, as well. Have fun with this recipe!

1 head cauliflower, chopped
4 parsnips, peeled and cubed
3 tablespoons organic, unsalted butter or ghee
1 tablespoon avocado oil
Sea salt and ground pepper, to taste
2 slices of bacon, uncured applewood smoked, diced
1 medium yellow onion, diced
2 celery stalks, chopped
1 large carrot, peeled and chopped
2 beefsteak tomatoes, roughly chopped
3½ ounces shiitake mushrooms (or preferred mushrooms), roughly chopped
2 teaspoons Worcestershire sauce
1 tablespoon fresh thyme leaves
1 pound ground beef
½ pound ground pork
½ pound ground bison
6-ounce can organic tomato paste
1 large egg

Fill medium pot halfway with salted water. Add cauliflower and parsnips. Bring to boil. Lower heat to medium and cook until cauliflower and parsnips are fork tender (approximately 30 minutes). Drain and add to a mixing bowl. Add butter, avocado oil and salt and pepper, to taste. Blend until smooth. Set aside.

Preheat oven to 350°F.

In a 12-inch skillet, place bacon, onion, celery, carrots, tomatoes, mushrooms, Worcestershire sauce, thyme, salt and pepper. Cook on medium, until onions are translucent and veggies are tender. Add ground meat and tomato paste. Cook, on medium, until meat is browned. Bring to boil and cook for 10 minutes, allowing juices to boil off.

Spoon meat mixture into a baking dish (smaller if you like thicker layers or larger is you like thinner layers). Spread cauliflower mixture over the meat mixture. Whisk egg in a separate bowl. Brush over the top of the cauliflower layer.

Bake 30 minutes. Broil for an additional 5 minutes to brown. Let rest for 20 minutes. Serve.

Enjoy!

Buffalo Shoulder Roast & Black Truffle Mashed Parsnips

I saw this wonderful piece of shoulder and had to cook it. I had made bison burgers and grilled buffalo for a salad, but had never done a roast. Just like any roast, I assumed low and slow was the key to cooking this wonderful meat. I was right… no knife needed for this meal!

Roast:

2 tablespoons bacon grease

2-pound buffalo shoulder roast

2½ cups beef broth

1 tablespoon Worcestershire sauce

1 large onion (chunked)

4 garlic cloves, peeled and quartered

3 large carrots, peeled and cut in ½-inch lengths

Sea salt and ground pepper

Mashed Parsnips:

4 large parsnips, peeled and largely cubed

3-4 garlic cloves, peeled

3 tablespoons organic, unsalted butter or ghee

1 teaspoon black truffle oil

Sea salt and ground pepper, to taste

Fresh chopped parsley (optional)

In a heavy-bottomed pot or cast-iron pan, heat the bacon grease on medium-high heat. With a paper towel, pat the roast dry and season liberally with sea salt and ground pepper. Place the roast in the heated pan and sear on each side (about a minute per side). Remove from pan. Place in slow cooker.

In the original pot or pan, add broth, Worcestershire sauce, onion, and garlic cloves. Heat on medium for 10 minutes, scraping the "brown bits" from the bottom of the pan. Pour over the meat in the slow cooker. If the liquid does not cover the top of the meat, add enough water to do so. Cook, on low, for 5 hours. Add carrots. Cook for an additional 2 hours.

Bring a pot of salted water, parsnips, and garlic cloves to a boil. Reduce to medium-low heat and cook until parsnips are fork tender.

Drain. Transfer to a bowl. Add butter and truffle oil. Blend until smooth. Salt and pepper to taste.

Slice roast. Serve with mashed parsnips, carrots, and onions from the slow cooker. Pour a little of the juice over the plate. Garnish with parsley.

Enjoy!

 Cavegirl Tip If you cannot find Black Truffle Oil, please feel free to substitute with the many flavored oils on the market today.

Prosciutto-Wrapped Poppers & Honey Mustard

Poppers:
8-10 jalapenos
¼ pound sweet Italian sausage, loose or removed from the casings
4 ounces thinly sliced prosciutto

Dipping Sauce:
¼ cup yellow mustard
4 teaspoons raw honey
½ teaspoon apple cider vinegar

Cilantro, chopped (optional)

Preheat oven to 350°F.

Cut the tips off of the jalapenos. Using a paring knife, cut out the "ribs" on the inside of each pepper. Using a small spoon, or the handle of the spoon, carefully hollow out each pepper. Once hollowed out, rinse removing all seeds.

Stuff each jalapeno with sausage. Wrap each stuffed pepper with a piece of prosciutto. Place jalapenos on a broiling pan (or some type of pan to allow the juices from the sausage to drip).

Cook for approximately 30 minutes.

Combine dipping sauce ingredients and refrigerate covered until ready to use.

Remove poppers from oven. Cool 10 minutes. Plate and garnish with chopped cilantro. Serve with sauce.

Yield: 8-10 poppers

Enjoy!

Bacon-Wrapped Chorizo Stuffed Dates

My husband and I went to a wonderful restaurant in Louisville, Kentucky, on Valentine's Day. They have an AMAZING appetizer that I dream about. Their version utilizes goat cheese. However, I thought it would still be wonderful "paleotized", by eliminating the cheese and replacing it with my own sauce. This is an incredibly easy, yet rich and luxurious treat. The combination of flavors ~ the sweetness of the dates, the spiciness of the sausage, the richness of the bacon and the smokiness in the tomato sauce ~ is an explosion of wonderful.

¼ pound loose chorizo
10 large Medjool dates
5 slices applewood smoked
    bacon, nitrate-free
1-2 chipotle peppers, in adobo
    sauce, strained (found in the
    international section of your
    local grocery store)
½ cup of your favorite
    marinara/pasta sauce

Preheat oven to 425°F.

Slice each date lengthwise, on each side, to remove pits.

Sauté chorizo in a skillet, over medium heat, approximately 5 minutes, until thoroughly cooked. Set aside on a paper towel-lined plate.

Cut bacon slices in half. Line a baking pan with parchment paper.

Stuff dates with sausage. Wrap ½ piece of bacon around each stuffed date. Place the bacon, seams down, on parchment paper.

Bake 20-25 minutes (depending on the size of your dates) or until bacon starts to crisp.

In a food processor, add the chipotle(s) and the marinara sauce. Blend. Transfer to a small pot and warm, on medium heat. Do not boil.

Spoon sauce onto a plate. Place dates on the sauce.

Yield: 10 stuffed dates

Enjoy!

B.A.T. Crazy Lettuce Wraps
(bacon, avocado, tomato)

6 Bibb lettuce cups

1 avocado

2 slices nitrate-free thick cut bacon

2 Roma tomatoes, seeded and diced

Sea salt and ground pepper (optional)

Roma tomatoes are my favorite to use for wraps because of their flavor and minimal seeds.

Dice your avocado or mash it and spread it on each lettuce leaf.

Add a little salt and ground pepper, and chomp away...

Variation: I think a chopped hard-boiled egg would be good in this, too.

Yield: 6 lettuce wraps

Enjoy!

 Cavegirl Tip   Thick cut bacon is the key to this wrap!

This is super easy and very flexible. Use whatever veggies are available in your refrigerator. Next time, I'm going to do zucchini strips and onion slices! This is good as a side, snack, lunch or even an appetizer. Get creative and have fun!

4 asparagus spears
4 bell pepper strips,
   about ¼ inch thick
4 slices of bacon, nitrate-free

Preheat oven to 350°F.

Snap off the bottoms of the asparagus spears.

Cut the bacon strips lengthwise. Spiral-wrap two long strips of bacon around 1 asparagus spear and 1 bell pepper strip. Repeat for all of the spears and pepper combinations.

Bake 40 minutes.

Enjoy!

Asparagus has a natural soft spot, which meets a tough end. When snapped here, the tough end of the asparagus can be easily removed. No knives or cutting involved.

Ratatouille Topped Spaghetti Squash & Tomato Salad

Spaghetti Squash:
2 small spaghetti squash
1-2 tablespoons avocado oil
  (or preferred cooking oil)
Garlic salt and ground pepper, to taste

Ratatouille:
1 tablespoon organic, unsalted butter
  or ghee
1 small onion, diced
2-4 garlic cloves, peeled, minced
2 cups diced eggplant
1 cup diced yellow squash
½ cup diced orange bell pepper
1 cup diced zucchini
1 cup chopped mushrooms (any variety)
2 cups diced tomatoes
2 tablespoons chopped fresh basil
1 tablespoon Italian seasoning
Sea salt and ground pepper, to taste

Tomato Salad:
A mix of heirloom tomatoes, the quantity
  depends on your preferred salad size
Extra virgin olive oil
Balsamic vinegar, high quality, low sugar
Sea salt and ground pepper, to taste

Preheat oven to 375˚F.

Cut the spaghetti squash in half, lengthwise.
Place, skin-side down, in a baking dish. Brush squash halves lightly, with avocado oil. Season with salt and pepper.
Bake 45 minutes, until squash easily breaks away from the edges, with a fork.

Cool for 10 minutes. Scoop out the flesh with a fork into a bowl. Set aside.

While the squash are cooking, place ratatouille ingredients into a 12-inch skillet, on medium heat, for 20 minutes, stirring occasionally.

Plate squash and top with ratatouille mixture. Plate heirloom tomatoes, on the side. Drizzle desired amount of olive oil over the tomatoes. Drizzle the balsamic vinegar over both.
Season with salt and pepper, if necessary.

Serves 4-6

Enjoy!

 Cavegirl Tip
If dairy is within your dietary allowances, this is a great meal to add some freshly shaved Parmesan cheese, as a garnish.

"Fried" Eggplant Marinara
(on a bed of greens)

1 medium eggplant
2 large eggs
2 cups almond meal
1 tablespoon macadamia nut oil (or oil of choice)
Sea salt and ground pepper, to taste
1 cup marinara sauce
4 cups of arugula (or, greens of choice)

Preheat oven to 400˚F.

Line two cookie sheets with parchment paper.

Peel eggplant and slice into ¼-inch rounds.

Whisk eggs in a medium bowl. Place almond meal in another bowl. Dredge each eggplant round in eggs and then coat with the almond meal on each side. Place on parchment paper.

**Drizzle or mist the oil over the coated rounds.
Salt and pepper lightly.**

Bake 30 minutes.

**Place a cup of greens on each plate. Top with eggplant.
Pour a ¼ cup of marinara sauce over each serving.**

Yield: 3-4 servings

Enjoy!

Eggplant & Prosciutto Rollatini

Rollatini Filling:
5 ounces cremini mushrooms
   (or preferred mushroom)
½ avocado
1 tablespoon avocado oil
¼ cup marinara sauce
3 basil leaves, fresh
2 garlic cloves
½ teaspoon sea salt

8 thin slices of eggplant,
   cut lengthwise
4 ounces prosciutto
   (8 thin slices)
2 cups marinara

Preheat oven to 350°F.

Place the first 7 ingredients into food processor. Blend into a paste. If necessary, add more marinara. Set aside.

In an 8x8-baking dish, place ½ cup marinara sauce.

For rollatini: Place a slice of eggplant on your working surface. Spread some of your rollatini filling over the slice. Next, layer a slice of prosciutto. Roll up from the larger end to the smaller. Place the roll seam side down into the baking dish. Repeat eight times. Pour remaining marinara over the rolls.

Bake 45 minutes. Remove from oven. Cool 10-15 minutes.

Yield: 8 rollatini

Enjoy!

By Sea

By Sea

24 littleneck clams

2 tablespoons organic
  unsalted butter or ghee

½ medium onion, diced

6 garlic cloves, peeled and
  chopped

½ cup dry white wine

1 cup chicken broth

1 cup diced tomatoes

¼ chopped flat leaf parsley

Sea salt and ground pepper,
  to taste

½ cup basil, chiffonade
  (cut into long, thin strips)

In a large saucepan, melt butter over medium heat. Add onions and garlic. Stir occasionally, until onions are translucent.

Add white wine and chicken broth. Bring to boil.

Add clams, tomatoes, parsley, salt, and pepper. Cover. Reduce heat to medium-low. Cook 9 minutes, until clams open. Note: If a clam doesn't open, discard it.

Garnish with fresh basil.

Enjoy!

 For some added dimension and bulk, add precooked sausage to the saucepan before adding the clams.

Crab Legs with Parsley Lemon Butter

My oldest daughter is allergic to shellfish. However, crab legs are my youngest daughter's favorite food. So, one day when my oldest daughter was at a sleepover, my youngest daughter and I couldn't resist making this simple masterpiece!

3 pounds of crab legs

½ cup fresh parsley
6 tablespoons organic, unsalted butter or ghee, melted
1 small lemon, juiced
¼ teaspoon sea salt

Bring a large pot of water to a boil. Add crab legs. Simmer for approximately 6 minutes, on low heat. Drain and set aside.

In a food processor, blend remaining ingredients. Serve immediately.

Serves 2-3

Enjoy!

This is a very light, mayonnaise-free, salad. Just a couple of leftover small lobster tails (½ cup of meat) helped make this a perfect lunch. This recipe would also be great with tuna or salmon.

½ cup lobster meat
(approximately 2 small
lobster tails)
1 stalk celery, finely chopped
2 tablespoons small diced
avocado
1½ teaspoon Dijon mustard
1 tablespoon capers
1 tablespoon fresh dill
1 Roma tomato, chopped
1 teaspoon fresh lemon juice

Sea salt and ground pepper,
to taste
3-4 Bibb lettuce leaves
Extra virgin olive oil (optional)

**In a bowl, toss first eight ingredients.
Season with salt and pepper.**

Spoon into the lettuce bowls.

Optional: Spritz or drizzle with olive oil. Serve.

Serves 1-2

Enjoy!

Scallops & Citrusy-Garlic Greens

2 pieces of nitrate-free bacon
8-10 sea scallops
2 handfuls of spinach, arugula, or preferred greens
3-4 garlic cloves, minced
1 tablespoon freshly-squeezed orange juice

In a large skillet, cook bacon. Set aside and crumble when cooled.

Using a paper towel, pat the scallops dry. This will help give them good color and a nice sear. Place scallops in the heated skillet and cook for 3 minutes. Flip and cook for an additional 1-2 minutes, depending on their thickness. Remove the scallops from the skillet. Set aside.

In the same skillet, place greens, garlic, and orange juice. Cook on medium until the greens are wilted. Plate greens. Add scallops and garnish with bacon.

Serves 2

Enjoy!

The epitome of a Paleo appetizer! Protein (shrimp) + fat (avocado) + yummy produce, creating perfection! I love the name of this recipe, too! Shrimp Guac-Tail will impress your Paleo and non-Paleo friends alike!

1 pound shrimp, extra large (26-30 count) peeled and deveined

Guacamole:
2 avocados
2 garlic cloves, peeled and minced
1 teaspoon Sriracha (or preferred hot sauce)
1 large Roma tomato, seeded and diced
Juice from one small lime
1 teaspoon sea salt
2 tablespoons fresh cilantro (optional)

In a medium saucepan, fill halfway with water. Boil. Add shrimp. Boil 2 minutes, until opaque. Drain. Set aside.

Cut avocados in half. Discard skins and inner seed. Mash avocado "meat" roughly with a fork.

Add lime juice first, to avoid browning of avocado. Add remaining ingredients. Mix gently with a spoon. Distribute guacamole and shrimp evenly among plates. Garnish with cilantro.

Yield: 10 appetizer cups

Enjoy!

Caribbean Coconut Shrimp

4 tablespoons organic, unsalted butter or ghee
1 large shallot, minced
6 cloves of fresh garlic, minced
½ cup organic tomato sauce
13.5-ounce can of coconut milk
3 stalks lemongrass, first two layers removed and discarded, inner core chopped
⅓ cup cilantro, chopped
Sea salt & ground pepper to taste
1½ pounds shrimp, deveined and raw (51-60 count)
¼ cup unsweetened coconut flakes, toasted

Preheat oven to 350°F.

In a medium saucepan, heat butter, shallot and garlic, until shallots are tender and butter is melted. Add tomato sauce, coconut milk, lemongrass, cilantro, salt, and pepper. Stir slowly, until blended, allowing the tomato sauce to warm.

Place shrimp in an 8×8 baking dish. Pour coconut milk mixture over the shrimp. Bake uncovered for 25 minutes.

Spoon the shrimp into bowls and garnish with toasted coconut and additional chopped cilantro.

Serves 4

Enjoy!

 Serve this recipe over some "riced" cauliflower.

Deconstructed Spring Roll Salad

This was originally going to be an actual spring roll, with the cucumber slices forming the exterior. However, it was a failed endeavor. There was no way that I was going to let all of my prep work and great ingredients go to waste; hence the "deconstructed" part. Fortunately, this "happy accident" turned out to be a very fresh and vibrant salad.

12 ounces shrimp, Large (31-35 count), peeled and deveined

3.2-ounce container of shiitake mushrooms

½ lemon, squeezed for juice

1 avocado, finely diced

1 large cucumber, peeled and ends removed

1 large carrot, peeled and cut into matchsticks

1 mango, finely diced

½ cup cilantro, chopped

Dressing:

¼ cup toasted sesame oil

Juice of 1 lime

1 tablespoon plum vinegar

2 tablespoons raw honey

5 macadamia nuts, raw

2 teaspoons Sriracha

1 teaspoon sea salt

½ knob of ginger (about 1 tablespoon), peeled

2 cloves of garlic, peeled

Put all of the dressing ingredients in a food processor (or blender). Puree and refrigerate.

In a medium saucepan, boil water. Add shrimp and resume boiling for 1-2 minutes, until opaque. Remove shrimp and set aside. Reserve water.

Bring water to a boil again. Add shiitake mushrooms and boil for 3 minutes. Drain. Set aside.

Squeeze lemon over diced avocado, to avoid browning. Set aside.

Use a mandolin to thinly slice the cucumber (this can be done by hand). Rotate cucumber a quarter turn when you hit the inner seeds. Do this to all four sides.

Plate all of the salad ingredients in sections. Either drizzle dressing over your salad or serve on the side for dipping.

Serves 4

Enjoy!

Shrimp & Mushroom Stir-Fry

1 tablespoon sesame oil

1 pound shrimp, medium-large
(36-40 count), peeled and
deveined

5 ounces shiitake mushrooms

4 scallions, chopped

1 carrot, peeled and chopped

1 yellow squash, chopped

2 cloves garlic, peeled, minced

1 tablespoon freshly grated
ginger

¼ teaspoon sea salt

2 tablespoons coconut aminos

Heat sesame oil on medium-high heat. Add remaining ingredients. Sauté 2 minutes. Cover and continue cooking, 5 minutes. Remove lid. Toss and sauté another 5 minutes, allowing some of the juices to steam off.

Yield: 2-3 servings

Enjoy!

1 lemon

10 calamari tubes

¼ pound loose chorizo (or casings removed for links)

⅓ cup crabmeat

1 large egg

1 tablespoon almond meal/flour

Pinch of sea salt

1 shallot, finely diced

10 toothpicks

Avocado oil (or preferred oil)

1½ cups canned organic crushed tomatoes

1 teaspoon raw honey

Sea salt & ground pepper to taste

Garnish with chopped chives, parsley, or cilantro

Juice lemon in a small bowl. Place calamari tubes in the lemon juice.

In a separate medium bowl, combine chorizo, crabmeat, egg, almond meal, pinch of salt, and shallot until blended. Place mixture in a plastic storage bag and cut off a corner. Pipe mixture into the calamari tubes. Seal off the ends of the calamari using toothpicks.

Heat a grilling pan (or grill) on medium-high heat. Brush the stuffed tubes with preferred oil and season liberally with salt and pepper.

Cook for approximately 7-8 minutes on each side until the internal temperature reaches at least 160°F.

While this is cooking, place crushed tomatoes and raw honey in a small saucepan. Add a pinch of salt if desired. Stir and heat on medium until warm.

Spoon tomato mixture on a plate. Remove toothpicks from calamari and arrange on the plate.

Garnish with optional herbs.

Enjoy!

Calamari Salad

I love, love calamari!! As a teen, my family and I lived in Naples, Italy, for two years. I often ate calamari "fritte" (fried) and "misto"(mixed) salad. My father was a sailor and would often take the calamari tentacles and stick them out of his nose and pretend a squid was attacking him! (True story!) Here's my Paleo tribute to calamari and my dad!

1 pound calamari rings (or buy the tubes and cut into rings)

1 tablespoon organic, virgin coconut oil

Pinch of sea salt

1 small onion, diced

2 teaspoons of grated horseradish

Pomegranate seeds, cucumber slices, and pine nuts for garnish

Greens of your choice (spinach, arugula, etc.)

Extra virgin olive oil and balsamic vinegar

Sea salt and ground pepper, to taste

Cook calamari, oil, salt, onion, and horseradish in a skillet over medium heat for approximately 5 minutes until onions are translucent and calamari are opaque.

Divide greens among 3-4 plates. Using a slotted spoon, divide skillet mixture and place over greens.

Garnish with pomegranate seeds, cucumber slices, and pine nuts. Drizzle oil and vinegar over plates. Season with salt and pepper if necessary.

Serves 3-4

Enjoy!

You can buy calamari already cut up. It's also sold in cleaned tubes where you just have to slice it into rings. If you choose to buy calamari whole, I'm warning you, it's a process preparing, but it can be done. If you choose the latter, there are several online videos to show you how. It really is an experience!!

Tuna Salad (mayo-free)

5-ounce can of tuna, drained

2 teaspoons of mustard (I used
   yellow mustard. But, Dijon
   works, if you want a kick!)

1-2 teaspoons of fresh lemon
   juice

1 tablespoon of freshly
   chopped dill

Sea salt and ground pepper,
   to taste

Combine all ingredients in bowl. Done!

**Alternative additions: capers, chopped celery,
chopped onion, and/or nuts**

**Round out this meal with some strawberries, walnuts,
½ hard-boiled egg, celery sticks, and mushroom slices.**

Serves 1

Enjoy!

Tuna Club Boats

5-ounce can of tuna, drained

2 teaspoons Dijon mustard

½ avocado, mashed

Sea salt and ground pepper,
   to taste

2 pieces bacon, cooked and
   crumbled

1 Roma tomato, seeded and
   diced

2 Romaine lettuce leaves

1 hardboiled egg, peeled and
   diced

1 celery stalk, diced

In a medium bowl, combine tuna, mustard, avocado, salt, and pepper. Fold in bacon, hardboiled egg, celery, and tomato.

Spoon into lettuce leaves. Eat like a taco.

Yield: 2 tuna club boats

Enjoy!

Cod & Mashed Broccoli
with Horseradish & Bacon

1 pound of fresh broccoli, cut
   down into pieces

3-4 cloves of garlic, peeled

1 tablespoon horseradish,
   peeled and grated

1 tablespoon extra virgin olive
   oil or bacon grease

1 tablespoon organic unsalted
   butter or ghee

4, 4-ounce cod fillets

Sea salt and ground pepper

3 pieces nitrate-free bacon,
   cooked and crumbled

Place broccoli and garlic in a pot of salted water. Bring to a boil. Reduce heat to medium and cook until the broccoli is fork tender. Drain. In large bowl, place drained broccoli and garlic. Add horseradish, olive oil, and butter. Blend until desired consistency. Set aside.

Using a paper towel, pat down the cod, to remove moisture. Season both sides of each fillet with salt and pepper. Place 1 teaspoon of bacon grease (or preferred oil) into a stovetop-grilling pan. Grill fillets, on medium-high, approximately 5 minutes per side, until opaque throughout.

Plate broccoli mash. Place a cod fillet atop the mash. Garnish with crumbled bacon and a little grated horseradish (optional).

Serves 4

Enjoy!

Mahi Mahi
with Spicy Crab Meat Hollandaise

4, 4-ounce Mahi Mahi fillets
Sea salt and ground pepper

Hollandaise Sauce:
2 tablespoons organic,
    unsalted butter or ghee
1 egg yolk, beaten
1 teaspoon water
1 teaspoon freshly squeezed
    lemon juice
½ teaspoon Sriracha
    (or preferred hot sauce)
⅓ cup lump crab meat

2 tablespoons chives, chopped
    into ¼-inch lengths
1 piece thick-cut bacon, diced
    and cooked

Place Mahi Mahi fillets on a parchment paper-lined baking dish, skin side up. Season with salt and pepper. Bake until fish is opaque (approximately 15 minutes, depending on the thickness of your fish).

Hollandaise: Place all ingredients (except for the crab meat and butter) in the top part of a double boiler (don't let the boiling water below touch the top pan). Slowly add butter. Stir continuously, until the butter melts and the sauce thickens. Add crabmeat. Stir.

Plate the fish. Drizzle the spicy crabmeat hollandaise onto fillets. Garnish with bacon pieces and chives.

Serves 2-4

Enjoy!

Honey Lime Salmon

Salmon fillets (as many as you
    want to cook)
1 tablespoon raw honey, per
    fillet
Fresh lime slices, (approximately
    2 per fillet)
Sea salt

Preheat oven to 350°F.

Brush fillets with honey. Season with salt. Place 2-3 lime slices on each salmon fillet. Bake until desired doneness, approximately 12-15 minutes. The cooking time will vary with the thickness of the fillet.

Enjoy!

Salmon-Stuffed Mushrooms

From lunching with the ladies to watching the CrossFit Games, this is a tasty, light bite!

12 ounces wild-caught salmon, cooked and flaked

¼ cup finely diced celery

2 tablespoons whole grain Dijon mustard

1 tablespoon small capers, drained

1 tablespoon chopped fresh dill (or dried dill)

2-3 garlic cloves, peeled, minced

1 teaspoon ground celery seed

1 teaspoon cayenne pepper

1 teaspoon fresh horseradish

Sea salt and ground pepper, to taste

12 medium (approximately 3-inch diameter) mushrooms

1 tablespoon avocado oil (or preferred oil)

2 tablespoons fresh lime juice (optional)

Smoked paprika (optional)

Chopped fresh dill (optional)

Preheat oven to 350°F.

In a bowl, combine first ten ingredients until the ingredients are well combined.

Clean mushrooms and remove stems. Then, mist or brush avocado oil onto the mushrooms. Stuff each mushroom with salmon mixture. Place stuffed mushrooms in a 9x13 baking dish.

Bake 20 minutes. Remove from oven. Cool.

Optional Garnish: Squeeze ½ of a lime over mushrooms. Sprinkle with smoked paprika and chopped fresh dill.

Yield: 12 stuffed mushrooms

Enjoy!

Soups & Stews

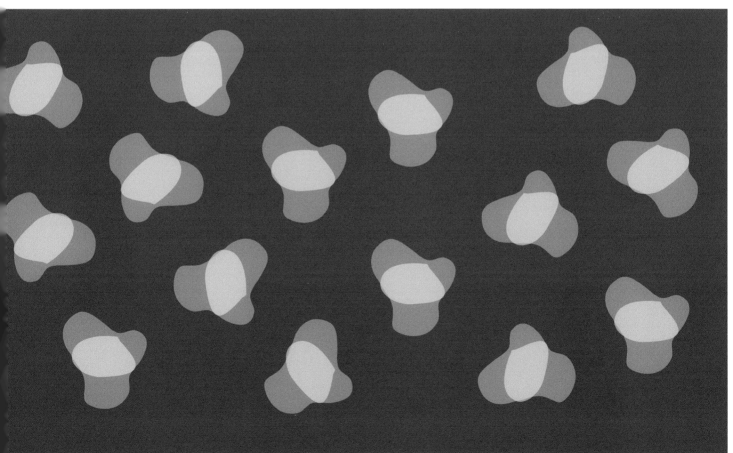

Soups & Stews

Creamy Roasted Tomato Soup

One summer morning, while shopping at our local farmer's market for a new soup recipe, I found some beautiful tomatoes. Here is a soup inspired by my find!

4 pounds tomatoes (any variety)
1 large leek, trimmed and roughly chopped
3 cloves elephant garlic, peeled, halved
Almond oil (or preferred oil)
Ground pepper and sea salt to taste
6 cups chicken broth
5 tablespoons organic, unsalted butter or ghee
2 tablespoons Italian seasoning
1 tablespoon Sherry
½ cup organic heavy cream (optional)
Basil, about 10 leaves

Preheat oven to 350°F.

Cut medium and large tomatoes in half or quarters. Smaller tomatoes can be left whole.

In a large baking dish, place the tomatoes, leeks, and garlic cloves. Drizzle with oil. Season with pepper and salt. Bake 40 minutes.

To large pot, over medium heat, add broth, butter, Italian seasoning, and 4 basil leaves. Add tomatoes, Sherry, and optional cream. Simmer, on low heat, 30 minutes. With an immersion blender, puree soup, until smooth. Season with salt (optional).

Serve warm with a basil garnish (cut chiffonade).

Serves 4-6

Enjoy!

Savory Butternut Squash Soup

Ingredients to Roast:
3 pounds butternut squash,
   peeled and seeded
   (set seeds aside, but do
   not discard)
5 garlic cloves, peeled, minced
2 apples, peeled and cored
1 leek, chopped
oil of choice + sea salt to season

Stovetop:
1 leek, chopped
2 carrots, peeled and chopped
2 celery stalks, chopped
4 tablespoons organic, unsalted
   butter or ghee
1 teaspoon ground celery seed
½ teaspoon cinnamon
1 teaspoon ground pepper
1 teaspoon sea salt
6 cups chicken broth

Additional ingredient:
1 teaspoon Sriracha
   (or preferred hot sauce)

Preheat oven to 350°F.

In a gallon plastic bag, place butternut squash, garlic, apple, leeks, salt, and oil. Shake to distribute the oil. Place ingredients in a large baking dish. Bake for 60 minutes.

In a Dutch oven or heavy-bottomed pot, add chopped leek, carrots, celery, butter, celery seed, cinnamon, pepper, and salt. Sauté, on low heat, for 20 minutes, until veggies are tender.

Add 6 cups of chicken broth to pan. Scrape brown bits off of the bottom of the pan and stir.

Add baking pan ingredients to pot.

Using the used greased baking pan, add butternut squash seeds, Sriracha and 1 teaspoon sea salt. Bake at 200°F for 30 minutes.

Use immersion blender to cream soup. Stir.

Garnish with baked squash seeds.

Serves 4-6

Enjoy!

Cauliflower & Pear Soup

3 tablespoons unsalted organic, unsalted butter or ghee
1 large onion, diced
1 carrot, peeled and diced
2 stalks of celery, diced
5 cups chicken broth
1 head of cauliflower, roughly chopped (stems removed)
2 red pears, peeled, cored and sliced
2 teaspoons smoked paprika
1 teaspoon dill
1 teaspoon fresh lemon juice
1-2 bay leaves
Sea salt and ground pepper, to taste
1 tablespoon cooking Sherry

Optional Cream Garnish:
¼ cup organic heavy whipping cream
½ teaspoon smoked paprika
1 teaspoon fresh lemon juice
¼ teaspoon sea salt

In a heavy-bottomed pot or Dutch oven, over medium-high heat, add butter, onion, carrot and celery. Sauté, until onions are translucent. Add chicken broth and cauliflower. Bring to a boil. Reduce to low heat and simmer. Add pears, paprika, dill, lemon juice, salt, pepper and bay leaf. Simmer, approximately 20 minutes, until cauliflower is fork tender.

Remove bay leaf. Using an immersion blender, blend, until smooth. Add Sherry, salt, and pepper.

Remove from heat. Set aside.

Optional cream garnish: Whisk garnish ingredients, on high, until medium stiff peaks form.

Serve soup in bowls. Top with a dollop of cream.

Additional toppings: strips of fresh pear, chives, sprinkle of paprika

Serves 4-6

Enjoy!

Loaded Fauxtato Soup

This is GOOD! The taste resembles a comforting potato skin appetizer. I hope you like this as much as we did!

---

1 head organic cauliflower
4 cloves of garlic
1-2 tablespoons almond oil
3 tablespoons organic, unsalted butter or ghee
1 yellow onion, roughly chopped
3 celery stalks, chopped
1 tablespoon dried oregano
1 slice of applewood smoked bacon, finely diced
6 cups chicken broth
¼ cup organic heavy cream (optional)
2-3 teaspoons sea salt
1 teaspoon ground pepper
Fresh parsley, chopped (for garnish)
6 slices of applewood bacon, chopped (for garnish)

Preheat oven to 350°F.

Chop cauliflower into chunks. Place cauliflower and garlic into a baking dish. Drizzle with 1-2 tablespoons of almond oil. Bake, uncovered, 30 minutes. Remove from oven. Set aside.

In a Dutch oven or heavy-bottomed pot on medium heat, saute butter, onion, celery, oregano, and bacon until onions are translucent.

Add cauliflower, garlic, broth, salt, and pepper. Bring to a boil. Reduce heat and simmer, uncovered, 15 minutes.

Using an immersion blender directly in the pot, blend soup until smooth. (alternative method: Blend pot ingredients in batches in a stand blender and pour back into the pot).

**Add optional cream. Continue to simmer for 15 minutes.
In the meantime, cook the remaining 6 slices of bacon until crisp. Set bacon aside on a paper towel-lined plate.**

Garnish with crumbled bacon and chopped parsley.

Serves 5-6

Enjoy!

Broccoli & Bacon Soup

I have a confession. The bowl strictly inspired this soup. My husband thinks it's an ugly bowl. By the way, the soup is amazing ~ no cream necessary here. The parsnip gives it a full-bodied smooth texture.

12 ounces nitrate-free bacon, uncooked, roughly diced

6 ounces nitrate-free bacon, cooked and crumbled

1 medium onion, roughly chopped

1 large parsnip, peeled and diced

1 large carrot, peeled and diced

3-4 garlic cloves, peeled and quartered

2 celery stalks, chopped

6 cups chicken or turkey broth

1½ pounds fresh broccoli, chopped

1 teaspoon sea salt

1 teaspoon freshly ground pepper

In a heavy-bottomed pot, over medium heat, fry bacon. Add onion, parsnip, carrot, garlic, and celery. Stir, completely coating vegetables. Continue cooking for approximately 10 minutes.

Add broth. Stir. Add broccoli, salt, and pepper. Bring to a boil. Reduce heat and cover. Simmer for 30 minutes.

Using an immersion blender, blend soup until smooth. If you do not have an immersion blender, transfer soup in batches to a standing blender and process until smooth. Salt, to taste.

Serve and garnish with crumbled bacon.

Serves 6-8

Enjoy!

Hearty Ham & Fauxtato Soup

I asked my girls to come up with the soup of the week and they requested Ham and Potato. I said, "Uh, no!!"
But I told them that we could have fauxtatoes (parsnips)!! This soup is hearty and comforting.

1 cup + 2 cups diced ham
2 tablespoons bacon grease
1 onion
2 celery stalks
1 cup mushrooms (any variety)
4 cloves of garlic, peeled
6 cups chicken broth
1 tablespoon sea salt
1 teaspoon ground pepper
2 shakes of Tabasco®
   (or preferred hot sauce)
4 cups (about 5-7) parsnips,
   peeled and diced
2 teaspoons fresh thyme leaves
   (plus more for garnish)
½ cup organic heavy cream
   (optional)

In a thick-bottomed pot, melt bacon grease.
Add 1 cup of ham and brown.

Either dice the onion, celery, mushrooms, and garlic, or place them in a food processor and pulse until chopped. Add to the pot, scraping the pan for flavor. Sauté, until tender. Add chicken broth, Tabasco®, parsnips and thyme. Bring to a boil. Simmer for 30 minutes, over low heat, until parsnips are tender.

Using an immersion blender, blend mixture until almost smooth ~ I like mine a little chunky. (This can be done in batches in an upright blender. Then, return to pot.) Add remaining 2 cups of diced ham and cream. Stir.

Simmer for minimum one hour. Add salt and pepper (optional).

Serve in bowls. Garnish with fresh thyme leaves.

Serves 4-6

Enjoy!

Crab, Bacon & Parsnip Chowder

Chowder is traditionally served with potatoes; however, your guests will never know that you subbed in parsnips. Both are root veggies and have similar textures. However, parsnips have a slightly lower glycemic index than white potatoes.

16 ounces lump crab meat, NOT imitation

5 thick pieces of applewood smoked bacon

6 cups broth of your choice

1 pound parsnips, peeled and diced

2-4 cloves of garlic, peeled

4 celery stalks, chopped

1 small bell pepper (color of choice), seeded and diced

1 teaspoon Sriracha (or preferred hot sauce)

1 tablespoon Old Bay® Seasoning

1 tablespoon fresh thyme

1 fresh bay leaf

½ red onion, diced

2 tablespoon coconut flour

1 tablespoon arrowroot powder

8 ounces organic heavy cream (optional)

3 tablespoons cooking Sherry

In a medium pot, over medium heat, add 3 cups of the broth, half of the parsnips and the garlic cloves, until parsnips are fork-tender. Use an immersion blender or regular blender to puree. Set aside.

In a separate pot, over medium heat, add remaining broth, remaining parsnips, celery, bell pepper, Sriracha, Old Bay®, thyme, and bay leaf. Reduce to medium-low heat and simmer.

Chop bacon into ½-inch slices. Fry in a skillet, until almost crispy. Set aside on a paper towel-lined plate. Remove all but about a tablespoon of the bacon grease from the skillet. Add onion to skillet. Transfer a ladle of broth from the simmering pot, to the skillet. Whisk in the coconut flour and arrowroot, scraping all of the bits from the pan as you stir. Transfer mixture to your simmering pot.

Add pureed mixture to your simmering pot. Stir. Add cream (optional), crab, and bacon. Simmer on low for 30 minutes. Add sherry. Remove bay leaf. Serve.

Serves 4-6

Enjoy!

Cioppino

This is a truly versatile soup. Use different seafoods to create a new dish every time!

2 halibut steaks (about 12 ounces),
    cut into 1-inch cubes
1 pound shrimp, peeled and deveined
1 pound mussels, rinsed and de-bearded
12 ounces sea scallops
4 tablespoons organic, unsalted butter
    or ghee
1 medium onion, diced
1 celery stalk, chopped
1 green pepper, diced
1 small fennel bulb, diced
5 cloves of garlic, peeled, minced
1 tablespoon fresh thyme leaves
1 tablespoon fresh oregano, chopped
1 teaspoon sea salt
½ teaspoon ground pepper
Pinch of saffron
¼ teaspoon cayenne pepper
28-ounce can organic, diced tomatoes,
    including juice
1 cup bottled clam juice
2 cups chicken or veggie broth
2 bay leaves
1 cup dry red wine
Juice of 1 navel orange
Fresh basil, chiffonade (optional)

In a Dutch oven or a thick-bottomed pot, add butter, onion, celery, green pepper, fennel, garlic, thyme, oregano, salt, pepper, saffron, and cayenne. Heat on medium, until onions are translucent.

Add tomatoes, clam juice, broth, bay leaf, wine, and orange juice. Bring to boil. Reduce to low heat and simmer.

Add mussels. Cook on medium for 5 minutes.
Add shrimp, halibut, and scallops. Cook for 6-7 minutes, stirring after 4 minutes. Discard bay leaves and any mussels that don't open.

Divide Cioppino into four or five bowls. Garnish with optional basil. Serve immediately.

Serves 4-5

Enjoy!

Lobster Bisque

1 pound lobster meat
  (about 5 small lobster tails)
3½ tablespoons organic,
  unsalted butter or ghee
2 cups chopped leeks
  (approximately 2 large)
2 celery stalks, chopped
2 carrots, peeled and large diced
½ head of cauliflower, roughly
  chopped
4 cups vegetable broth
2 cups water
1 tablespoon Herbes de Provence
  (or Italian seasoning)
Sea salt and ground pepper,
  to taste
1 bay leaf
4-6 garlic cloves, peeled
2 tablespoons cooking Sherry
6-ounce can organic tomato
  paste
Fresh thyme leaves, to garnish

Bring a large pot of salted water to a boil. Carefully drop in lobster tails. Cook for 5 minutes. Remove tails from water. Let cool.

Remove meat from shells. Set meat aside and roughly chop. Set large carcass parts/shells aside.

In a heavy-bottomed pot or Dutch oven, heat 2 tablespoons of butter, leeks, celery, and carrots on medium. Cook until leeks are tender.

Add cauliflower, broth, water, Herbes de Provence, salt & pepper, bay leaf, garlic cloves, and lobster shells. Bring to a boil. Reduce and simmer covered for 30 minutes.

Using a slotted spoon, remove shells and bay leaf. Discard. Using an immersion blender, blend pot ingredients until smooth. (An alternative is to transfer small batches to a stand blender, and blend until smooth).

Add approximately ¾ of the lobster meat back to the pot along with the cooking Sherry and tomato paste. Stir until combined and simmer.

In a small pan over medium heat, melt remaining butter and add remaining lobster. Cook for 2 minutes, until the lobster meat is coated.

Pour bisque into bowls. Garnish each bowl with the buttered lobster and fresh thyme leaves.

Serves 4

Enjoy!

Derby Day Burgoo

Burgoo??? What's that? It's a traditional soup/stew, originating in Kentucky, usually served the week of the Kentucky Derby. Traditionally, it is cooked in large iron kettles, using meat from that day's hunting expedition and veggies that were already on-hand around the house. Burgoo is never made the same way twice and is different from family to family. I thought I would throw in my Derby hat and give it a good Paleo try!

1½ pounds boneless, skinless chicken thighs, cubed
1 pound beef stew meat, cut into 1-inch pieces
2 tablespoons extra virgin olive oil
4 tablespoons organic, unsalted butter or ghee
4 stalks celery, chopped
2 cups asparagus cut into 1-inch lengths
1 red onion, chopped
4 cloves of garlic, peeled, roughly chopped
1 large parsnip, peeled and diced
1 large carrot, peeled and sliced half-moon style
4 cups chicken broth
4 cups beef broth
2 cups of crushed fresh tomatoes
15-ounce can of tomato sauce
1 cup cut okra (fresh or frozen)
3 tablespoons Worcestershire sauce
Sea salt and ground pepper, to taste

In a large heavy-bottomed pot, heat olive oil, over medium-high heat. Add chicken and beef. Occasionally, stir gently. The goal here is to get a good sear on all sides of the meat. Do not cook all of the way through. This process should take approximately 3 minutes. Spoon meat into a separate bowl. Set aside.

In the same pot, place butter, celery, asparagus, onion, garlic, parsnips, and carrot. Sauté on medium heat, until butter is melted and onions are tender. Add both broths to pot. Stir.

Add the remaining ingredients. Bring to a boil. Simmer, on low heat, for 3 hours.

Serves 8-10

Enjoy!

 As with most soups, this one is best served the second day!

This is football-season food! Depending on your "heat-o-meter" preference, play with the amount of chipotles and Sriracha you add. As the recipe stands, I would say this is about a 6 on a 10-point scale, with 10 being the hottest.

2 pounds lean ground beef
1 tablespoon extra virgin olive oil
1 medium onion, chopped
1 bell pepper (any color), chopped
10 ounces Baby Bella/crimini mushrooms, chopped
28-ounce can of diced tomatoes, in juice (do not drain)
28-ounce can plum tomatoes, whole and peeled (do not drain)
1 small can, fire roasted diced green chilies
1 chipotle pepper in adobo sauce, chopped
1 teaspoon adobo sauce (from the can of chipotles)
1 teaspoon Sriracha (or preferred hot sauce)
½ teaspoon paprika
1 teaspoon chili powder
1 teaspoon sea salt
2 tablespoons fresh chopped cilantro (extra, for garnish)

In a large skillet, over medium heat, add olive oil, ground beef, onion, bell peppers and mushrooms, until onions are translucent and beef is browned.

In a heavy-bottomed large pot, over medium heat, add both cans of tomatoes, including their juices, and remaining ingredients.

Transfer skillet mixture to the pot.

Bring to boil. Reduce heat and simmer (one hour minimum).

Garnish with fresh cilantro.

Serves 6-8

Enjoy!

Bacon Jam Meatballs in Brodo

One day I made a delicious Bacon Jam (page 121). As it was cooking, I thought that it would make a great meatball ingredient. When I lived in Naples, Italy they had a dish called Tortellini in Brodo (tortellini in broth). I thought that these meatballs would make a great substitute. I was right... especially with fresh, chopped basil leaves sprinkled on top.

Meatballs:
1 pound ground beef
¼ cup Bacon Jam (page 121)
1 large shallot, finely chopped
¼ cup almond meal
1 large egg

Broth:
5 cups beef or chicken broth
5 tablespoons fresh basil,
   chopped

In a large mixing bowl, combine meatball ingredients. Form into 16 meatballs.

Lightly grease a baking pan with preferred oil. Arrange meatballs on the pan. Bake 25-30 minutes.

Heat broth and divide into four bowls. Place four meatballs in each bowl. Garnish with basil and serve.

Yield: 16 meatballs

Enjoy!

Cabbage & Kielbasa Soup

2 tablespoons organic, unsalted butter or ghee

1 pound parsnips, peeled and cubed

1 large onion, diced

1½ pounds smoked kielbasa sausage, thinly sliced on a diagonal

1 large carrot, peeled and chopped

2 celery stalks, diced

5 cups chicken broth

14.5-ounce can of diced tomatoes, juice included

3 tablespoons fresh chopped dill (an extra tablespoon needed for optional garnish)

1 teaspoon garlic powder

1 teaspoon ground coriander

½ teaspoon smoked paprika

½ teaspoon ground celery seed

½ head of cabbage, thinly sliced and chopped

Sea salt and ground pepper, to taste

In a heavy-bottomed pot, over medium heat, add the butter, parsnips, onion, kielbasa, carrot, and celery. Sauté, until onions are translucent, stirring occasionally.

Add chicken broth and tomatoes. Bring to boil for 5 minutes, while adding the remaining ingredients. Stir. Simmer covered on low for 1 hour.

Add fresh dill to each bowl for garnish.

Serves 5-7

Enjoy!

Spicy Chicken Chili

1½ pounds ground chicken
2 tablespoon organic,
     unsalted butter or ghee
1 large onion, diced
1 parsnip, peeled and diced
8 ounces white mushrooms,
     quartered
2 celery stalks, diced
1 carrot, peeled and sliced
3 cups chicken broth
3-5 garlic cloves, peeled and
     minced
1 jalapeno, finely diced (seeds
     and inner white spine
     removed)
2 teaspoons chili powder
¼ teaspoon red pepper flakes
1 tablespoon dried oregano
Sea salt and ground pepper,
     to taste

Cook ground chicken in a skillet and set aside.

Melt butter in a heavy-bottomed pot. Add onion, parsnip, mushrooms, celery, and carrot and cook on medium until onions are translucent. Add remaining ingredients, including the cooked chicken.

Bring to a boil. Reduce and simmer for another hour or two to give the flavors time to marry together. Add more salt and pepper to taste, if necessary.

Optional Toppings:
- Fresh cilantro leaves
- Whisk a few tablespoons of organic whipping cream.
   Add a dollop to each bowl of soup replacing the
   traditional sour cream.
- Fresh lime slices

Serves 4

Enjoy!

Chicken "Noodle" Soup

If you don't have a vegetable spiraler yet, run out and buy one. It's a kitchen gadget you will actually enjoy and use.

2 cups chicken breast, cooked and diced

2 tablespoons organic, unsalted butter or ghee

1 onion, chopped

2 carrots, peeled and thinly sliced

2 celery stalks, chopped

1 bay leaf

4 cups chicken broth

2-3 garlic cloves, peeled, minced

1 tablespoon fresh thyme leaves, removed from stem

Sea salt and ground pepper, to taste

1 medium turnip, peeled

In a large heavy-bottomed pot, over medium heat, add chicken, butter, onion, carrots, celery, and bay leaf, until onions are translucent.

Add broth, garlic, thyme, salt and pepper. Bring to boil. Reduce heat and simmer 30 minutes.

Spiral the turnip. Roughly cut "noodles" onto 1-inch lengths. Add to stock. Simmer 5 minutes. Ladle into bowls.

Serves 4

Enjoy!

Mushroom & Chicken Soup

My daughter saw a can of this flavor in the soup aisle and wanted to make it. The chicken adds protein and another level of flavor to an already wonderful soup!

1 stick organic, unsalted butter or ghee
2 cups chopped Vidalia (sweet) onion
2 stalks of celery, chopped
3 cloves garlic, peeled, minced
5 cups chicken broth
1 tablespoon Italian seasoning
Sea salt and ground pepper (optional)
10 ounces button mushrooms, roughly chopped
10 ounces Baby Bella/crimini mushrooms, roughly chopped
½ cup organic heavy cream (optional)
1 tablespoon cooking Sherry
2 cups chicken breast, cooked and cubed

In a large pot, over low heat, add butter, onions, celery, and garlic, until butter is melted and onions start to become translucent.

Add broth, Italian seasoning, salt, pepper, and mushrooms.

Bring to a boil. Reduce to medium heat and let simmer approximately 5 minutes. Reduce to low heat. Blend until smooth, with emersion blender. Add cream, Sherry, and chicken. Stir. Simmer 15 minutes.

Add salt and or pepper, if desired.

Serves 4-6

Enjoy!

This & That
(sauces & more)

This & That (sauces & more)

Nut meal or flour is quite easy to make. I use different nuts for the varieties of flavor they each lend to a dish. I keep the flour/meal in jars, in my pantry. This makes them ready to use, when needed.

To make your own: Place nuts in a food processor or blender. Chop until desired consistency. That's it!

Nut meal refers to a chunkier consistency. This is great in cookie recipes. To achieve this, don't pulse in the food processor as long.

Nut flour has a finer consistency. Pulse the nuts a little longer in the food processor to achieve. I prefer nut flour when "breading" fish, chicken, and vegetables before baking. Just make sure you don't pulse for too long or it will turn into a paste.

Mash it Up!

From left to right: broccoli, parsnip, sweet potato, cauliflower

To mash: On the stovetop, place roughly chopped vegetables (I added a couple cloves of garlic to the parsnips) in a pot of salted water. Bring to a boil. Reduce to medium heat and let cook, until fork tender. Drain water. Transfer to a mixing bowl. Blend until desired consistency, with preferred spices and oils.

 Be sparing with the oils. It doesn't take much to help along the "mash" process. The rest is just for flavor. Remember to taste as you go, too!

Below is what I used; but don't be afraid to try curries, celery salt, hot sauce, and flavored oils.

Broccoli: horseradish, salt/pepper, avocado oil, and ghee.

Parsnip: rosemary infused olive oil, ghee, sea salt, and ground pepper.

Sweet Potato: ground cinnamon, ghee, and a dash of organic whipping cream.

Cauliflower: ghee, sea salt, ground pepper, and extra virgin olive oil. Hand-stir in some crispy bacon, at the end.

Enjoy!

First, note that there are three different factors that can be changed with vinaigrette:

1. Type of oil: Although wonderful, extra virgin olive oil (EVOO) is not the end all, be all. There are many other "safe" varieties to use, in Paleo cooking; avocado oil, pumpkin oil, flavored olive oils, sesame oil and black truffle oil, for instance.
2. Type of vinegar: Balsamic vinegar is yumilicious (make sure you pick a low sugar version) but there are other flavor options, too. One of my favorites is fig balsamic vinegar. I also found rosemary-Infused vinegar at my farmer's market over the summer. Other varieties include, but are not limited to, apple cider vinegar (ACV), white wine vinegar, and cabernet vinegar.
3. Additions to your oil and vinegar: The options are as endless as your spice rack!

 For vinaigrettes, stick to 3 parts oil to 1 part vinegar. After that, go crazy.

Below are some suggested additions to your oil and vinegar. Just whisk into oil and vinegar before serving:

1. **Dijon mustard**
2. **Dijon mustard and a little warmed raw honey**
3. **Fresh dill (great added to a salmon salad vinaigrette)**
4. **Minced garlic**
5. **Sriracha (hot sauce for a kick!)**
6. **Sesame oil, white wine vinegar, fresh ginger, garlic, a squeeze of fresh orange juice and scallions**
7. **A slice or two of cooked bacon; heat chopped shallots in the bacon fat, cracked pepper (perfect over spinach)**
8. **Fresh horseradish and garlic (excellent over a steak salad)**
9. **Curry spice (a nice compliment to slaws)**
10. **Fresh basil (great for almost anything!)**

Enjoy!

Beet Horseradish

⅓ cup peeled and grated
   horseradish root
⅔ cup peeled and grated beet
   (about 1 medium)
1 tablespoon red wine vinegar
1 tablespoon organic coconut
   palm sugar

Combine all ingredients together.

Refrigerate, until ready to serve.

Yield: 1 cup

Enjoy!

 I love this served atop a good steak. It starts off sweet, but after a couple of bites... look out! It has a bit of a kick to it.

½ cup canned, organic, tomato sauce

¼ cup tomato paste

1 tablespoon whole grain mustard

1 tablespoon pure maple syrup

2-3 cloves of garlic, peeled, minced

1 teaspoon Worcestershire sauce

2 teaspoons hot sauce

¼ teaspoon sea salt

¼ teaspoon lemon juice

Whisk all ingredients together. Refrigerate for up to 10 days.

Yield: approximately ¾ cup

Enjoy!

Avocado Pico de Gallo

1½ cups Roma tomatoes,
   seeded and diced
3-4 cloves of garlic, peeled and
   minced
Juice of 1 lime
1 small onion, diced
¼ cup fresh cilantro, chopped
1 avocado, diced
1 jalapeno, seeded, spines
   removed, diced

Mix all of the ingredients in a bowl.

Season with sea salt and ground pepper.

Yield: approximately 3 cups

Enjoy!

 Serve this with cubed, cooked chicken in lettuce leaves, creating a "wrap", or atop a salad.

⅓ cup finely diced Vidalia onion

6-ounce can organic tomato paste

1 + ⅓ cups chicken broth

⅛ teaspoon ground chipotle chili (or cayenne pepper)

1 teaspoon chili powder

¼ teaspoon sea salt

½ teaspoon dried oregano

½ teaspoon dried parsley flakes

2-3 cloves garlic, peeled, minced

In a saucepan, over medium-high heat, add onion, tomato paste and 1 cup chicken broth and stir.

Add remaining ingredients (except for the additional chicken broth) and continue to cook for another 2-4 minutes, stirring between additions. If the sauce is too thick add more chicken stock, a little at a time. Remove from heat. Use immediately or refrigerate in an airtight container for up to 3 days.

Yield: approximately 1½ cups

Enjoy!

Salsa Verde

¾ pound tomatillos, husks
   removed
2 large shallots, quartered
3-4 garlic cloves, peeled
   and quartered
1 Anaheim chili pepper,
   seeded and diced
1 teaspoon sea salt
1 tablespoon fresh lime juice
1 tablespoon Sriracha
   (or preferred hot sauce)
½ cup fresh cilantro, roughly
   chopped

Place husked tomatillos in a skillet over medium heat. Sauté, until sides are browned. Set aside.

Add all ingredients into a food processor or blender. Blend, until well combined and chunky.

Refrigerate for at least 2 hours and until ready to serve.

Yield: approximately 2 cups

Enjoy!

Cavegirl Guacamole

A good starter base for any guacamole creation. For example, if you really like heat, add more hot sauce or chopped jalapenos. If you're afraid of vampires, pile on the garlic (that's me)!

2 avocados
Juice from one small lime
2 garlic cloves, peeled and
   minced
1 teaspoon Sriracha
   (or preferred hot sauce)
1 large Roma tomato, seeded
   and diced
1 teaspoon sea salt
2 tablespoons fresh cilantro

**Squeeze lime juice into a small mixing bowl.
Cut avocados in half and scoop out flesh, discarding inner seed and skin. Smash with a fork against the side of bowl (having the lime in the bowl will also help to keep the avocado from browning). Add remaining ingredients. Toss gently. Refrigerate covered. Serve when ready.**

Yield: approximately 1½ cups

Enjoy!

Cavegirl Marinara

7-8 ripe large Roma tomatoes, quartered

1 large red pepper, seeded and diced

1 tablespoon avocado oil (or preferred oil)

2 teaspoons sea salt

4-6 cloves of garlic, peeled and chopped

1 celery stalk, chopped

1 red onion, diced

¼ cup basil, chopped

¼ cup fresh oregano leaves

2 tablespoons Italian seasoning

1 teaspoon red pepper flakes

2 teaspoons balsamic vinegar

Sea salt and ground pepper, to taste

Add first nine ingredients to a heavy-bottomed pot or Dutch oven. Sauté, covered, over medium heat, until vegetables become tender and tomatoes start to break down (approximately 15 minutes). Stir in Italian seasoning, red pepper flakes, and balsamic vinegar.

Using an immersion blender, blend pot ingredients, until smooth. Or, transfer pot ingredients, in batches, to a stand blender and puree. Return to pot.

Bring mixture to a boil. Reduce to low heat, and simmer, uncovered, I hour, allowing sauce to thicken and flavors to meld. Remove from heat. Add salt and pepper, to taste.

Yield: approximately 3 cups

Enjoy!

Cocktail Sauce

I LOVE cocktail sauce! I thought it would be fun to make my own. It's great with boiled shrimp. The recipe calls for many ingredients. However, most are already in your pantry. It can be served immediately. I prefer making it a day ahead, allowing all of the flavors to mingle and come to life.

6-ounce can organic tomato paste
1 tablespoon white wine vinegar
½ teaspoon Dijon mustard
2 tablespoons raw honey
1 teaspoon sea salt
¼ teaspoon celery seed
⅛ teaspoon garlic powder
⅛ teaspoon cayenne pepper
⅛ teaspoon ground cinnamon
⅓ cup water
3-4 tablespoons horseradish (taste as you go as this is a spicy preference item)
1 teaspoon lemon juice
½ teaspoon Worcestershire sauce

Combine all ingredients and mix well. Add extra salt or horseradish tweaking it to your preferred taste.

Refrigerate overnight for best results.

Yield: approximately ¾ cup

Enjoy!

Spiced Paleonnaise

2 egg yolks
¼ teaspoon cayenne pepper
Pinch of fine sea salt
3-4 garlic cloves
2 teaspoons lemon juice
½ cup mild extra virgin olive oil

Add egg yolks, cayenne, salt, garlic, and lemon juice to a food processor or blender and pulse until frothy. Slowly add the oil, a teaspoon at a time, blending continuosly. Serve immediately, or refrigerate up to a week.

Yield: ¾ cup

Enjoy!

 When the recipe states to add the oil slowly, really take this to heart. This will make or break your mayonnaise. Patience is your friend on this one. I know from experience!

Bacon Jam

I originally wanted something interesting to put atop my un-bunned burger. After smelling the wonderfulness coming from the slow cooker, I had a vision of this mixed in with ground beef before forming meatballs... maybe even on the side of my morning scrambled eggs. The possibilities are endless!

18 ounces uncured applewood-smoked bacon, quartered

2 medium onions, roughly chopped

3-4 cloves of garlic, peeled and chopped

¼ cup apple cider vinegar

¼ cup pure maple syrup

2 chipotles, in adobo sauce, chopped

1 teaspoon of adobo sauce from the chipotles

½ teaspoon smoked paprika

3 tablespoons maple sugar crystals (or coconut crystals)

1 tablespoon instant coffee crystals

1 cup water

Fry bacon in a skillet, until medium crispness... don't overcook. Remove and place on a paper towel-lined plate. Reserve 1-2 tablespoons of bacon grease. Discard the rest.

In a medium pot, heat bacon grease. Add onions and garlic. Sauté, until onions are opaque. Add remaining ingredients, including the bacon, stirring between the additions of each ingredient. Bring to a boil. Remove from heat and transfer to a slow cooker. Cook, on low heat setting, 3 hours. Using an immersion blender, blend mixture, until desired consistency (I like mine a little chunky). If the mixture gets too thick, just add a little water, one tablespoon at a time. Continue to cook, on low, for 1 hour.

Transfer mixture into a sealed container. Use immediately or refrigerate.

Yield: approximately 3 cups

Enjoy!

Mango Pesto

This fresh pesto pairs well with fish or chicken.

½ cup diced mango
½ cup Italian parsley
¼ cup basil leaves
½ cup raw pecans
2 garlic cloves, peeled
1 tablespoon extra virgin
  olive oil
½ teaspoon coconut aminos
Pinch of sea salt
½ teaspoon Sriracha
  (or preferred hot sauce)
1 tablespoon fresh lemon juice

Place all ingredients in a food processor and blend, until smooth (yep, it's that easy).

Refrigerate.

Yield: approximately 1 cup

Enjoy!

1 cup fresh mint leaves
1 cup fresh parsley leaves
¼ medium onion, roughly chopped
⅓ cup pine nuts
2-3 garlic cloves, peeled
5 tablespoons extra virgin olive oil
1 teaspoon lemon zest
1 teaspoon sea salt

Place all ingredients in a food processor and blend until smooth. Refrigerate. Use within 5 days.

Yield: ¾ cup

Enjoy!

Pickled Bell Peppers

2 bell peppers (color of choice, sliced in strips)
1 cup apple cider vinegar
1 cup water
3-5 cloves of garlic, peeled and quartered
1 small jalapeno, seeded and diced
1 teaspoon black peppercorns
½ teaspoon ground coriander
½ teaspoon ground celery seed
1 teaspoon sea salt
¼ cup coconut palm sugar crystals

Combine ingredients in a lidded container. Stir.

Refrigerate for at least 24 hours and up to two weeks.

Serve with burger patties, on salads, or eat them right out of the jar! Also, get creative using cucumbers or other vegetables!

Enjoy!

Sides

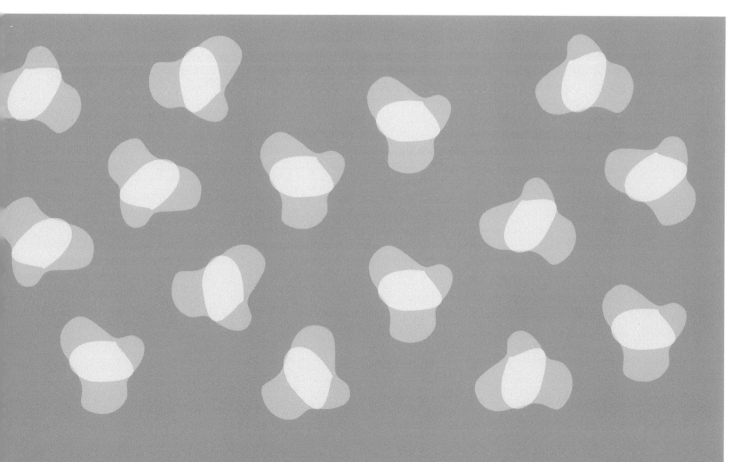

Sides

Squash Casserole

Being from Georgia, we always had squash casserole for Thanksgiving. It was one of my favorites! When I was pregnant with my second child, I craved squash casserole and I made it once a week. The traditional recipe calls for cheese and bread; however, I don't miss the cheese in this version. I used almond meal to replace the breading, too.

- 4 cups yellow squash (about 2 large), thinly sliced (I used a mandolin)
- 4 large eggs
- 1 tablespoon organic, unsalted butter or ghee, melted
- 2 tablespoons organic heavy cream
- 4 tablespoons almond meal
- 1 teaspoon sea salt
- 1 leek, use the bottom third along with some of the green, thinly sliced

Preheat oven to 350°F.

In a medium bowl, beat eggs. Add butter, cream, 3 tablespoons almond meal, salt, and beaten eggs. Add sliced squash to mixture and coat.

In a 7×7-baking dish, layer overlapping squash slices for a thick first row. Add a thin layer of leeks. Repeat with remaining squash and leeks.

Pour the remaining liquid over the casserole.
Sprinkle 1 tablespoon almond meal on top.

Bake, uncovered, 50 minutes or until egg mixture is firm.
Remove from oven. Cool 30 minutes before slicing and serving.

Serves 6-8

Enjoy!

Broccoli Coleslaw

1 cup Paleonnaise (page 120)
1 cup broccoli matchsticks
  (cut from the stems)
½ large carrot, julienned
¼ cup chopped radicchio
1 tablespoon raw sunflower
  seeds (plus another
  tablespoon for garnish)
½ cup quartered seedless red
  grapes
2 tablespoons finely diced red
  pepper
1 tablespoon chopped fresh
  parsley leaves (plus another
  tablespoon for garnish)
Sea salt and ground pepper,
  to taste

Make Paleonnaise. Set aside in the refrigerator.

Prepare and combine remaining ingredients, in a medium bowl. Stir in Paleonnaise, until all slaw is coated.

Refrigerate for at least ½ hour to meld flavors.

Garnish with additional sunflower seeds and parsley.

Yield: approximately 2 cups

Enjoy!

A lot of stores sell a precut 10-ounce organic mix of cut broccoli, carrots, and red cabbage made exclusively for coleslaw. It's a quick grab and cuts down on your prep time.

Broccoli Casserole

I've eaten broccoli casserole every Thanksgiving my entire life and was feeling it was time to give this recipe a makeover! This version has no cheese (unlike the original); however, I didn't really miss it. Also, the recipe traditionally calls for cracker crumbs on the top layer. Instead, I sprinkled a little almond meal to replicate the crunch. I hope you like this one!

5 cups fresh broccoli (about a head and a half), chopped and steamed
1 cup Paleonnaise (page 120)
2 large eggs
½ medium onion, chopped
⅛ cup almond meal

"Condensed" Mushroom Soup:
8 ounces button mushrooms (or mushrooms of choice), quartered
1 celery stalk, sliced
1 tablespoon organic, unsalted butter
1 small parsnip, peeled and diced
Sea salt and ground pepper, to taste
1 cup chicken broth
1 teaspoon cooking Sherry

Preheat oven to 350°F.

In a medium saucepan, add mushrooms, celery, butter, parsnip, salt, pepper, and chicken stock. Heat, on medium-high, until parsnips are tender. Add Sherry. Using an immersion blender, blend until smooth (or use a stand blender or food processor). Set aside.

Combine steamed broccoli, Paleonnaise, eggs, mushroom soup, and onion. Spoon into a greased 8 x 11.5 pan. Sprinkle with almond meal.

Bake uncovered for 35 minutes, or until center is firm. Cool 15 minutes.

Serves 6-8

Enjoy!

Fauxtato Salad

1 pound parsnips, peeled and
    cubed
12 ounces nitrate-free bacon,
    diced
1 tablespoon capers
2 scallions, chopped
1 tablespoon whole grain Dijon
    mustard
2 tablespoons fresh dill
1 teaspoon fresh ground
    pepper
¼ cup Paleonnaise (page 120)

Place parsnips in a medium-sized pot. Fill with enough water
to cover parsnips. Cook, uncovered, on medium-high for
approximately 25 minutes, until the parsnips are fork tender.
Drain. Set aside.

Fry bacon, until crispy. Set aside on a paper towel-lined plate.

Combine all ingredients. Refrigerate minimum 30 minutes
before serving.

Serves 4-5

Enjoy!

Savory Sweet Potato Waffle Bread

Do you miss eating bread with your meal? This "bread" makes a wonderful addition to any meal!

3 cups peeled, grated,
   sweet potatoes
   (approximately 1 large)
1 medium onion, finely diced
   (about 1 cup)
5 large eggs
⅓ cup almond meal
1 teaspoon gluten free
   baking powder
1 teaspoon baking soda
1 teaspoon red pepper flakes
1 teaspoon sea salt
¼ cup sifted coconut flour
Oil or melted organic, unsalted
   butter or ghee (to brush on
   waffle iron)

Preheat waffle maker.

In a large mixing bowl, combine all ingredients.

Brush waffle iron with oil, butter, or ghee. Spoon mixture into waffle iron. Close lid and cook for approximately 6 minutes, until crisp. Note: If you are using a regular waffle machine, not a Belgian waffle maker, the cook-time may be decreased. Belgian waffles are thicker.

Remove waffle. Repeat.

Cut each waffle into quarters. Serve with meal.

**Yield: 5 Belgian waffles or 20 pieces of waffle bread,
      once cut to size**

Enjoy!

 Change up the spices or add herbs to this recipe to be compatible with any meal!

"Thai"ce Baked Sweet Potatoes

2 medium sweet potatoes
¼ teaspoon red curry paste
1 teaspoon freshly grated
  ginger
5 tablespoons unsweetened
  coconut milk
2 tablespoons organic,
  unsalted butter or ghee
Pinch of sea salt
Chives, chopped (optional
  garnish)

Preheat oven to 400°F.

Pierce sweet potatoes several times with a fork. Place in a baking dish and cook for approximately 40 minutes, until tender. Remove from oven and cool.

Reduce heat to 350°F.

Cut the potatoes lengthwise and scoop out the orange flesh, keeping the skins intact. Place flesh into a mixing bowl with remaining ingredients. Blend until smooth.

Place potato skin halves in a baking dish. Distribute sweet potato mixture among the skins.

Bake uncovered for 10 minutes.

Garnish with chives.

Serves 4

Enjoy!

Deviled Guac Eggs

Avocados are nature's mayonnaise. They add a rich creaminess; this is my take on deviled eggs! Great for Easter, parties, sides or just because!

1 dozen large eggs,
　　hard-boiled and peeled
2 tablespoons fresh cilantro,
　　chopped
Juice from ½ lime
1-2 cloves of garlic, peeled
1 ripe avocado
1 teaspoon Sriracha
　　(or preferred hot sauce)
Sea salt and ground pepper
5-6 grape tomatoes, thinly
　　sliced

Hard-boiled eggs: Place the eggs in a pot and fill with water just above the eggs. Bring to a boil. Cover. Reduce to a simmer, over low heat, 12 minutes. Immediately pour out hot water and replace with cold water. I also gently put a large glass of ice into the pot. This process makes egg peeling much easier.

Slice eggs in half. Place the egg-white halves on a plate. In a medium bowl, combine, egg yolks, 1 tablespoon cilantro, lime juice, garlic, avocado, Sriracha, salt, and pepper, until smooth. Place into a piping bag. Distribute filling among the eggs Place one tomato slice on top of each egg. Garnish with remaining chopped cilantro.

Yield: 24 deviled eggs

Enjoy!

If you do not have a piping bag, simply fill a plastic sandwich or gallon bag with the mixture and cut the tip off of a corner to desired thickness. Squeeze mixture into eggs. Alternatively, you can simply spoon the mixture into the egg halves.

Braised Fennel with Bacon

3 pieces of bacon, finely
chopped
4 scallions, sliced, including
a portion of the greens
1 fennel bulb, sliced (reserve
some of the top greens
for garnish)
1 teaspoon Sriracha
(or preferred hot sauce)
3-4 cloves of garlic, peeled
and minced
½ cup chicken broth

In a heavy-bottomed pot, partially fry bacon. Add scallions.
Continue frying 1 minute. Add remaining ingredients.

Bring to boil. Reduce heat to low, and simmer. Cover.
Continue cooking for 20 minutes. Salt and pepper to taste.

Garnish with snipped greens from the top of the fennel.

Serves 2-3

Enjoy!

Asparagus Casserole
(Green Bean Casserole Impostor)

This is in honor of an American Thanksgiving tradition, the Green Bean Casserole! I substituted the green bean pods with asparagus chunks... made a homemade condensed mushroom soup... baked the traditional fried onions, for the top... It's "Paleo-fied" and delicious!

"Fried" Onions:

2 small onions, thinly sliced
2 tablespoons avocado oil
   (or preferred oil)
¼ cup almond meal
½ cup arrowroot

"Condensed" Mushroom Soup:

8 ounces Baby Bellas (or
   mushroom of choice)
1 celery stalk, chopped
1 tablespoon organic,
   unsalted butter
1 small parsnip, peeled and
   diced
Sea salt and ground pepper
1 cup chicken broth
1 teaspoon cooking Sherry
2 bunches steamed asparagus,
   diced
¼ cup organic heavy cream
   (optional)

Toss 1 tablespoon oil and onions in a small bowl.

Preheat oven to 350°F.

Combine almond meal and arrowroot in a gallon plastic bag. Add oiled onions. Shake bag, coating onions. Set aside.

Brush 1 tablespoon of oil onto a baking dish. Distribute coated onions into baking dish. Bake, uncovered, 15 minutes. Stir. Bake for an additional 10 minutes. Stir. Bake 5 more minutes. (Onions will be somewhat crispy, some moister... that's okay because the rest will crisp later). Set aside.

In a medium saucepan, add mushrooms, celery, butter, parsnip, salt, pepper, and chicken broth. Heat, on medium-high, until parsnips are tender. Add Sherry. Using an immersion blender, blend until smooth (or use a stand blender or food processor). Add, heavy cream (optional). Stir.

Combine mushroom soup and asparagus. Pour into an 8x8-greased pan. Bake 15 minutes. Top with crispy onions. Bake 15 minutes. Cool 20 minutes, to thicken.

Serves 6-8

Enjoy!

Balsamic Strawberries

4 cups strawberries, stems trimmed, quartered

⅛ cup balsamic vinegar (high quality, low sugar)

1½ teaspoons coconut palm sugar (or sweetener of choice)

Toss ingredients together. Refrigerate 1 hour. Serve.

Yield: 4 cups

Enjoy!

Sweet Treats

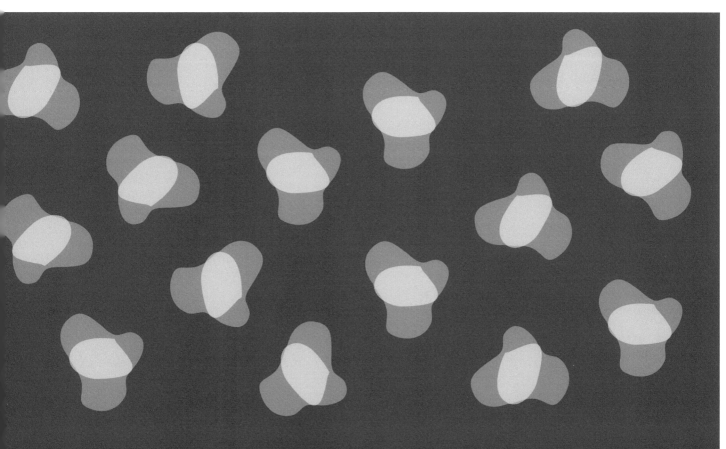

Sweet Treats

Maple Pear Tart

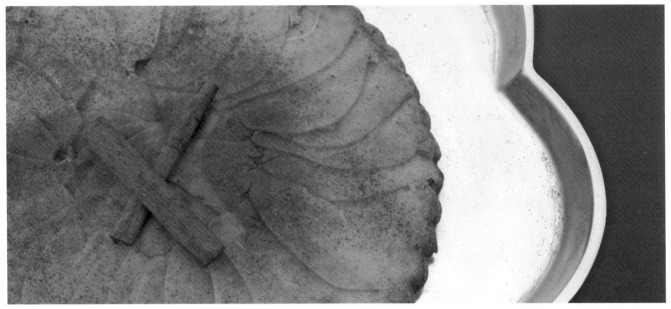

This started as upside-down mini pear cakes; however, the results weren't pretty. The second time around I experimented in a tart pan. Not only is the taste the same, but very pretty, too! This is GOOD, but I think it would be GREAT with a small scoop of Cinnamon Ice Cream (page 155), served on the side.

Cake portion:
3 large eggs
½ banana
⅛ cup coconut flour
⅛ cup creamy almond butter
2 Medjool dates, pitted and finely chopped
½ teaspoon pure vanilla extract
¼ teaspoon gluten free baking powder
½ teaspoon ground cinnamon
½ teaspoon pumpkin pie spice

Pears:
1 large Anjou pear (or your choice), cored and thinly sliced
¼ teaspoon ground cinnamon
1 teaspoon lemon juice
⅛ cup pure maple syrup
Pinch of sea salt

Preheat oven to 350°F.
Grease 9 x 1.125 inch tart pan.

Mix cake ingredients together. Set aside.

Combine pears, cinnamon, lemon juice, maple syrup, and sea salt in a pan over medium heat. Bring to boil. Gently stir. Reduce heat to low, simmer, until pears are tender (approximately 5 minutes). With a slotted spoon, scoop pears out of sauce and start overlapping pear slices on the outside perimeter of a tart pan. Once the outside circle is complete, overlap slices to form an inner circle.

Evenly spread cake mixture over pears.

Bake 20 minutes. Cool 10 minutes. Flip over onto a serving plate. Sprinkle with a little cinnamon (optional). Serve.

Enjoy!

 Cavegirl Tip For perfectly sliced pears, a mandolin is a great kitchen gadget to use.

Lemon Poppy Seed Cookies

3 tablespoons fresh lemon juice
1 tablespoon lemon zest (about 1 lemon)
1 tablespoon poppy seeds, plus extra for sprinkling
⅓ cup raw honey
½ cup creamy almond butter
½ cup coconut flour
1 large egg
1 teaspoon gluten free baking powder
½ teaspoon vanilla
Pinch of sea salt

Preheat oven to 350°F.

Line a cookie sheet with parchment paper.

In a bowl, blend all ingredients until smooth.

Spoon a tablespoon of batter and place on parchment paper about ½ inch apart. Take three fingers and press down to half the height. Sprinkle with more poppy seeds as desired.

Bake for 10 minutes. Let rest for 30 minutes.

Yield: 12-15 cookies

Enjoy!

Cranberry Apple Crisp

Just about any fruit or berry will work!

2 cups fresh cranberries
2 Granny Smith apples
   (approximately 3 cups),
   peeled, cored and diced
½ cup raw honey
½ teaspoon sea salt

Topping:
1 tablespoon unsweetened
   coconut flakes
½ cup walnuts, chopped
½ cup raw sunflower seeds
2 tablespoons creamy almond
   butter
1 tablespoon raw honey
1 teaspoon ground cinnamon

Preheat oven to 350°F.

Thoroughly combine cranberries, apples, honey, and sea salt, in a mixing bowl. Spoon onto a greased 8×8 pan.

In a separate bowl, combine "topping" ingredients. This mixture will be thick and lumpy. Gently stir until combined. Spoon small clumps of sticky topping mixture onto the cranberry-apple mixture.

Bake uncovered for 45 minutes. Remove from oven. Cool. Serve.

Serves 4-6

Enjoy!

Apple Pie Thumbprint Cookies

Cookie Portion:
¾ cup almond butter, unsalted, creamy
¼ cup coconut flour
¼ cup pecan meal (or preferred meal or nut flour)
1 teaspoon gluten free baking powder
1 large egg
2 teaspoons ground cinnamon
1 teaspoon pure vanilla extract
4 tablespoons organic coconut palm sugar

Topping:
¾ cup peeled, finely diced, Granny Smith apple
¼ cup pure maple syrup
1 teaspoon arrowroot
¼ teaspoon lemon juice

Preheat oven to 350°F.

In a mixing bowl, combine cookie ingredients, until blended.

Roll 12, 1-inch balls. With your thumb, press them down in the middle, on a parchment paper-lined cooking sheet. They will look like 12 small bowls. Bake 12 minutes.

Prepare your diced apples and place in a medium saucepan with remaining "topping" ingredients. Bring to a boil. Reduce to a simmer and cook, covered, 5 minutes.

When the cookies are done, remove from oven and distribute topping mixture over each cookie. Bake for an additional 3 minutes.

Cool COMPLETELY to let the cookies set.

Yield: 12 cookies

Enjoy!

Pumpkin Kiss Cookies

Cookies are an important food for many Paleo eaters and many non-Paleo eaters, too! Although I use raw honey in a lot of recipes, this one is sweetened with dates.

6 Medjool dates, pitted
¼ cup almond meal/flour
¼ cup pumpkin puree
1 large egg
½ teaspoon allspice
½ teaspoon ground cinnamon
1 teaspoon gluten free
     baking powder
¼ cup unsweetened coconut
     flakes
3.5 ounces dark chocolate
     (72% or higher)

Preheat oven to 350˚F.

In a food processor, blend dates and almond meal.

Combine pumpkin puree, egg, allspice, cinnamon, baking powder and coconut flakes in a medium sized mixing bowl with the date and almond meal mixture.

On a parchment paper-lined cookie sheet, drop about 2 teaspoons of batter, to form a ball, then push down in the center creating a "nest". Repeat with all batter.

Bake 10 minutes. Remove from oven and cool 10 minutes.

Melt dark chocolate in a double boiler, on low heat. Spoon melted chocolate into the center of each cookie. Cool for 1 hour.

Yield: 15 cookies

Enjoy!

Dark Chocolate Mint and Goji Berry Cookies

Many Cavegirl friends enjoy these cookies in their hiking packs ~ a lot of nutrition and energy ~ absolutely yummy!

1¼ cups almond or walnut meal

¼ cup coconut flour

3 tablespoons organic, unsalted butter, melted

¼ cup raw honey

¼ cup sunflower seeds

3.5-ounce dark chocolate bar (72% or higher), cut into small chunks

1 teaspoon peppermint extract

½ cup dried goji berries

1 teaspoon gluten free baking powder

Preheat oven to 350°F.

Line a cookie sheet with parchment paper.

Mix all ingredients until well-blended. Spoon tablespoons of batter about ½ inch apart.

Bake 10-12 minutes until slightly browned. Let rest for 20 minutes.

Yield: 20-22 cookies

Enjoy!

Trail Mix Cookies

1¼ cups walnut meal

3 tablespoons ghee or organic, unsalted butter

¼ cup raw honey

½ cup chopped dried cherries

3.5-ounce dark chocolate bar (72% or higher), cut into small chunks

1 teaspoon fresh orange zest

¼ cup unsweetened coconut flakes

2 tablespoons unsalted sunflower seeds

Preheat oven to 350°F.

Combine all ingredients so that the honey is well distributed. Line a baking sheet with parchment paper. Roll a tablespoon of cookie mix into a ball and place onto the baking sheet. Press down each ball. Leave about an inch between cookies. They will spread as they bake.

Bake 10 minutes. Cool for about 10 minutes, before transferring to a cooling rack. After transferring, cool for about another 30 minutes, to harden.

Yield: 20 cookies

Enjoy!

These cookies cook down very thin, almost like lace cookies. Make sure you really mix all of the ingredients well; otherwise you'll have pockets of honey bubbling out the sides of the cookies during the baking phase.

Chunky Chocolate Cookies

Just chunky goodness when you are craving something sweet!

¾ cup almond meal
¼ cup coconut flour
1 cup chopped pecans
¼ cup raw honey
3.5-ounce dark chocolate bar
(72% or higher), cut into
small chunks
1 large egg
1 teaspoon gluten free
baking powder

Preheat oven to 350°F.

Thoroughly combine all ingredients.

Place scoop of batter (approximately 2 teaspoonsful) on a parchment paper-lined cookie sheet, allowing 1-inch between cookies. Bake 10 minutes.

These cookies are crumbly when they first get out of the oven. Cool for about an hour, to firm them up, before serving.

Yield: 16-18 cookies

Enjoy!

Bacon Chocolate Meringues

4 egg whites,
    room temperature
2 teaspoons vanilla extract
¼ cup pure maple syrup
4 slices nitrate-free bacon
3.5-ounce dark chocolate bar
    (72% or higher)

Preheat oven to 200°F.

In a metal bowl, beat egg whites and vanilla until medium peaks form.

Slowly add maple syrup in a slow, steady drizzle as you continue to blend until stiff peaks form.

Spoon onto parchment paper-lined cookie sheets in teaspoonfuls. (Alternative: Use a pastry bag and wide tip or spoon into a gallon plastic bag and cut off the tip of one of the corners).

Cook for 2 hours. Turn the oven off, but let the meringues stay. Crack the oven door open and let the meringues rest in the oven for an additional 2 hours. Peel meringues off of the parchment paper.

Cook bacon until crisp and crumble when cooled. Set aside.

Melt chocolate over a double boiler. Dip the edge of a meringue in the chocolate. Sprinkle bacon on the chocolate. Place on a cooling rack. Repeat this with the remaining meringues.

Yield: 30 meringues

Enjoy!

Maple-Vanilla Meringues

4 egg whites,
  room temperature
2 teaspoons vanilla extract
¼ cup pure maple syrup

Preheat oven to 200° F

In a metal bowl, beat egg whites and vanilla until medium peaks form.

Slowly add maple syrup in a slow, steady drizzle as you continue to blend until stiff peaks form.

Spoon onto parchment paper-lined cookie sheets in teaspoonfuls. (Alternative: Use a pastry bag and wide tip or spoon into a gallon plastic bag and cut off the tip of one of the corners).

Cook for 2 hours. Turn the oven off, but let the meringues stay. Crack the oven door open and let the meringues rest in the oven for an additional 2 hours.

Peel meringues off of the parchment paper and store in an airtight container.

Yield: 30 meringues

Enjoy!

Macaroons
~ Dark Chocolate Dipped

½ cup organic heavy cream
½ cup unsweetened coconut
   flakes, firmly packed
¼ teaspoon almond extract
¼ teaspoon pure vanilla extract
¼ cup raw honey
⅛ teaspoon sea salt
1 large egg white
3.5-ounce dark chocolate bar
   (72% or higher)

Preheat oven to 350°F.

In a medium bowl, combine heavy cream, coconut, almond extract, vanilla extract, honey, and salt.

In a small bowl, whisk egg white, until medium-firm peaks form. Fold firm egg white into medium bowl ingredients.

Form 1-inch wide balls with your hands... pack them tightly together. Place on a parchment paper-lined cookie sheet. Bake 15 minutes. Remove from oven. Cool for 5 minutes, before transferring to a cooling rack. Cool an additional 10 minutes, on rack, before dipping into chocolate.

While macaroons are cooling, melt chocolate, in a double boiler, over low heat. Dip half of a macaroon in the melted chocolate. Place on a cooling rack.

Refrigerate, until ready to serve.

Yield: 16 macaroons

Enjoy!

Salted Caramel Ice Cream

Caramel:

2 tablespoon raw honey
½ teaspoon sea salt
¼ cup coconut cream
1 tablespoon organic, unsalted butter or ghee
¼ teaspoon pure vanilla extract

Ice Cream:

13.5-ounce can of coconut milk
¼ cup raw honey
1 vanilla bean, split lengthwise and seeds scraped
2 egg yolks

In a small saucepan, heat caramel ingredients, on low heat, for 5 minutes, until there is a low rolling boil around the edge of the mixture. Remove from heat. Set aside.

Over low heat, combine coconut milk, raw honey, and vanilla bean seeds. Whisk until everything is well blended. Remove from heat. Set aside.

Whisk 2 egg yolks in a separate bowl. Temper the yolks, to avoid cooking the eggs, by adding a small ladle of the ice cream mixture, stirring continuously. Add a second ladle, of ice cream mixture, to egg mixture. Once combined, pour this back into the saucepan. Stir. Add caramel mixture. Stir until combined. Refrigerate.

Follow the directions on your ice cream mixer for precise directions. I have owned several versions, and the general rule is to freeze the cavity overnight. I like to refrigerate the ice cream mixture covered for at least 3 hours, or overnight. Then, slowly add the mixture to the frozen cavity. After the mixture has blended for at least 30 minutes, transfer to a freezer-safe container. After 30-40 minutes, in the freezer, stir again.

Yield: approximately 1 pint

Enjoy!

Cavegirl Tip

I think the best stage of "Paleo ice cream" is after the 2-3 hours of freezing. After that, it becomes hard, due to the lack of actual cream. Timing is everything, but you won't be disappointed!

Lemon Ice Cream
with Blackberry Sauce

Ice Cream:
13.5-ounce can of coconut milk
¼ cup raw honey
2 teaspoons lemon extract
2 egg yolks

Blackberry Sauce:
5 ounces fresh or frozen
    blackberries
1 tablespoon pure maple syrup

Combine coconut milk and honey, in a medium saucepan, over low heat. Whisk. Add lemon extract. Stir.

Whisk 2 egg yolks in a separate bowl. Temper yolks, to avoid cooking the eggs, by adding a small ladle of hot mixture, stirring continuously. Add a second ladle to egg mixture. Once combined, pour this back into the saucepan and stir everything together. Refrigerate.

Follow the directions on your ice cream mixer for precise directions. I have owned several versions, and the general rule is to freeze the cavity overnight. I like to refrigerate the ice cream mixture covered for at least 3 hours, or overnight. Then, slowly add the mixture to the frozen cavity. After the mixture has blended for at least 30 minutes, transfer to a freezer-safe container. After 30-40 minutes, in the freezer, stir again.

For Blackberry Sauce:
In a small saucepan, over medium heat, combine blackberries and maple syrup, for approximately 5 minutes. Stir continuously. "Smoosh" blackberries against the side of the saucepan, forming a chunky blackberry liquid.

Drizzle blackberry sauce over ice cream and serve.

Yield: approximately 1 pint

Enjoy!

 For a fancy presentation, hollow out lemon halves and use as bowls.

Pear & Fig Ice Cream

12 black figs, ends trimmed

2 red pears, peeled, cored, and diced

2-3 tablespoons raw honey (taste for sweetness depending on your figs)

¼ cup water

13.5-ounce can coconut milk

1 teaspoon vanilla or 1 vanilla bean, split lengthwise and seeds scraped

2 large egg yolks

(Optional) Add one of these ingredients at the end of the mixing stage:

¼ cup finely diced crystalized ginger

¼ cup chopped nuts of choice

¼ cup dark chocolate chips

Place figs, pears, honey, and water in a medium saucepan over medium-high heat. Cook for about 8 minutes until the fruit starts to soften. Lower heat to low and continue to cook for approximately 20 additional minutes. Using a wooden spoon during the cooking time, break down the fruit until you have a slightly lumpy, thick mixture. Refrigerate for about an hour.

Place coconut milk, fig mixture, and vanilla in a medium saucepan over low heat. Whisk until well-blended. Remove from heat and set aside.

Whisk 2 egg yolks in a separate bowl. Temper yolks, to avoid cooking the eggs, by adding a small ladle of hot mixture, stirring continuously. Add a second ladle to egg mixture. Once combined, pour this back into the saucepan and stir.

Refrigerate until completely cooled.

Follow the directions on your ice cream mixer as each one may be a little different. Once your main mixture is blended, transfer to a freezing container/lidded bowl. Freeze. After 30-45 minutes, stir mixture again. I think the best stage of "Paleo ice cream" is after the first 1-3 hours of freezing.

Yield: approximately 1 pint

Enjoy!

Mint Dark Chocolate Chip Ice Cream

13.5-ounce can of coconut milk
¼ cup raw honey
1 teaspoon peppermint extract
2 egg yolks
2 ounces dark chocolate (72%
   or higher) Chocolate chips
   can be used for this recipe.
   Or, just chop up half of a
   dark chocolate bar.

Combine coconut milk and honey, in a medium saucepan, over low heat. Whisk. Add peppermint extract. Stir.

Whisk 2 egg yolks in a separate bowl. Temper yolks, to avoid cooking the eggs, by adding a small ladle of hot mixture, stirring continuously. Add a second ladle to egg mixture. Once combined, pour this back into the saucepan and stir. Refrigerate.

Follow the directions on your ice cream mixer for precise directions. I have owned several versions, and the general rule is to freeze the cavity overnight. I like to refrigerate the ice cream mixture covered for at least 3 hours before adding it to the frozen cavity.

Add chocolate about halfway through the blending process. After the mixture has blended for at least 30 minutes, transfer to a freezer-safe container. After 30-40 minutes, in the freezer, stir again.

Yield: approximately 1 pint

Enjoy!

Mocha Frappe Ice Cream

13.5-ounce can of coconut milk
2 teaspoons instant coffee
    crystals
¼ cup unsweetened cocoa
¼ cup raw honey
2 egg yolks

Place all ingredients (except for the yolks) in a medium saucepan over low heat. Whisk until everything is blended well together. Turn off heat.

Whisk 2 egg yolks in a separate bowl. Temper yolks, to avoid cooking the eggs, by adding a small ladle of hot mixture, stirring continuously. Add a second ladle to egg mixture. Once combined, pour this back into the saucepan and stir everything together. Refrigerate. Then, follow the directions on your ice cream mixer for precise directions.

Note: I have owned several ice cream mixers. The general rule is to freeze the cavity overnight. I like to refrigerate the ice cream mixture, covered, for at least 3 hours before slowly adding it to the frozen cavity. Transfer to a freezer-safe container. After 30-40 minutes, in the freezer, stir again. Freeze for at least 2-3 hours.

Yield: approximately 1 pint

Enjoy!

Cinnamon Ice Cream

So creamy and smooth! This ice cream pairs well with my Maple Pear Tart (page 139) and the Cranberry Apple Crisp (page 141).

13.5-ounce can of coconut milk
¼ cup raw honey
2 egg yolks
2 tablespoons ground cinnamon
1 teaspoon pure vanilla extract

In a medium saucepan, over low heat, combine coconut milk and honey. Whisk until blended. Add vanilla extract and cinnamon. Stir.

Whisk 2 egg yolks in a separate bowl. Temper yolks, to avoid cooking the eggs, by adding a small ladle of hot mixture, stirring continuously. Add a second ladle to egg mixture. Once combined, pour this back into the saucepan and stir everything together. Refrigerate. Then, follow the directions on your ice cream mixer for precise directions.

Note: I have owned several ice cream mixers. The general rule is to freeze the cavity overnight. I like to refrigerate the ice cream mixture, covered, for at least 3 hours before slowly adding it to the frozen cavity. Transfer to a freezer-safe container. After 30-40 minutes, in the freezer, stir again. Freeze for at least 2-3 hours.

Yield: approximately 1 pint

Enjoy!

Brownie Peppermint Sundae

Chocolate and peppermint ~ what's not to like? This is a kid-friendly recipe that's sure to be a family hit!
Note: This recipe takes a little patience in the construction... If you get frustrated or are short on time, just have a Peppermint Ice Cream Brownie Sundae, instead!

Brownie Portion:
1 cup walnut meal (ground up walnuts
   in a food processor)
¼ cup cocoa powder
1 large egg, whisked
¼ cup raw honey
1 teaspoon gluten free baking powder
¼ teaspoon baking soda
1 teaspoon bourbon vanilla
⅛ teaspoon sea salt
2 tablespoons coconut oil, melted

Peppermint Ice Cream:
13.5-ounce can of coconut milk
¼ cup raw honey
1¼ teaspoons peppermint extract
⅛ teaspoon butter extract
⅛ cup organic heavy whipping cream
   (optional)
2 egg yolks

Whipped Cream (optional):
1/4 cup organic heavy whipping cream
2 tablespoons coconut palm sugar crystals

Brownie Peppermint Sundae

Make Brownie Portion:

Preheat oven to 350°F.

Blend all of the brownie ingredients until smooth.

Although a greased 8×10 pan can be used, I used a brownie pan (kind of like a muffin pan with square partition 12-cavity bar pan). Evenly distribute the batter into your greased pan.

Bake 12 minutes. Remove from oven. Set aside.

Peppermint Ice Cream:

In a medium saucepan, over low heat, combine coconut milk and honey. Whisk until blended. Add peppermint extract, butter extract, and whipping cream (optional). Stir.

Whisk 2 egg yolks in a separate bowl. Temper yolks, to avoid cooking the eggs, by adding a small ladle of hot mixture, stirring continuously. Add a second ladle to egg mixture. Once combined, pour this back into the saucepan and stir everything together. Refrigerate. Then, follow the directions on your ice cream mixer for precise directions.

Whipped Cream:

For the whipped cream, using a stand or hand mixer, add cream and blend on medium-high. Slowly add coconut palm crystals while mixing to desired consistency.

Assemble sundaes.

Yield: 12 brownies and approximately 1 pint of peppermint ice cream

Enjoy!

 To achieve a pink color to your ice cream without using food coloring, add 1-2 tablespoons of beet juice from a can. It doesn't change the flavor and it adds a festive touch!

Jailhouse Rockin' Banana Boats

If Elvis were alive and kickin', this would be his Paleo go-to dessert!

1 banana
2 teaspoons almond butter
2 tablespoons unsweetened
   coconut flakes
2 egg whites, room
   temperature
1 tablespoon coconut palm
   sugar
2 ounces dark chocolate
   (72% or higher)
2 tablespoons chopped
   pecans

Slice banana lengthwise down the center. Place in two separate bowls. Spread almond butter down the length of each banana half. Sprinkle ½ tablespoon of coconut flakes on each half. Set aside.

Preheat broiler. Whisk egg whites in a metal bowl. Gradually add coconut crystals. Beat until you have stiff peaks, forming a meringue.

Spoon or pipe the meringue mixture alongside each banana half. Broil for 2-3 minutes until browned.

Remove from oven. Drizzle 1 ounce of melted chocolate over each banana/meringue. Top with crushed pecans and remaining coconut flakes.

Yield: 2 banana boats

Enjoy!

Almond Bark of Joy

Simple ingredients... easy to make... quick to disappear!

7 ounces 72% dark chocolate
1 tablespoon coconut butter
½ cup whole almonds, unsalted
¾ cup unsweetened coconut
    flakes

Line a baking sheet with parchment paper.

In a double boiler, slowly melt chocolate, until almost smooth. Add coconut butter, almonds, and coconut flakes. Stir, until chocolate is completely melted.

Spoon mixture onto parchment paper. Spread to about ¼-inch thickness.

Cool in the refrigerator for approximately 45 minutes.

Flip onto a cutting board and cut into desired sections. Refrigerate pieces (or freeze) until ready to eat.

Yield: approximately 10 pieces of bark

Enjoy!

Creamy Berry Pops

Berrylicious and refreshing!

¼ cup raw honey
1½ cups mixed berries, fresh or frozen
1 teaspoon pure vanilla extract
13.5 ounce can of coconut milk

In a small saucepan, over medium heat, add honey, berries, and vanilla. "Smoosh" the berries against the side of the pan while they are heating. Continue this action, until desired "chunkiness" is achieved. Remove from heat. Add coconut milk. Stir. Pour into ice pop molds (or paper cups with ice pop sticks).

Freeze overnight. Run warm water over the molds to release the ice pops.

Enjoy!

Melonsicles

Guilt-free summer indulgence!

2 cups watermelon, seeded, cubed
2 cups cantaloupe, seeded, cubed
5 fresh mint leaves
½ cup water

Blend all ingredients, until smooth. Pour into ice pop molds.

Alternative to store-bought plastic ice pop molds: Use small paper cups. Fill cups. Cover with a square of aluminum foil to stabilize an ice pop stick, until frozen.

Freeze overnight. Run warm water over the molds to release the ice pops.

Enjoy!

Jamocha Pops

13.5-ounce can of coconut milk
1 tablespoon instant coffee
   crystals
1 tablespoon unsweetened
   cocoa
¼ cup raw honey
1 teaspoon bourbon vanilla
   extract

Place all ingredients in a saucepan over medium heat, until the coffee crystals are dissolved. Stir occasionally.

Cool and pour into ice pop molds.

Freeze. Run warm water over the molds to release the ice pops.

Enjoy!

For the Kids

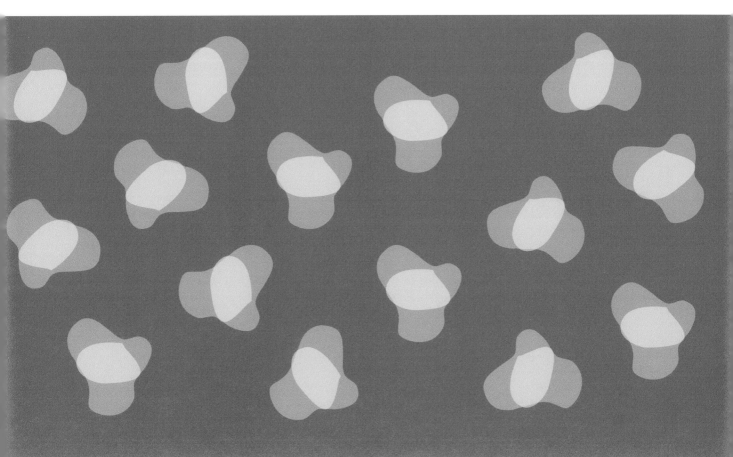

For the Kids

Steamed Artichokes with Sunshine Sauce

3 artichokes
2 lemon slices
1 garlic clove, peeled,
    cut in half
1 Bouquet Garni,
    or 1 tablespoon Italian
    Seasoning

Sauce:
½ stick of organic,
    unsalted butter
1 teaspoon Dijon mustard
¼ lemon, juiced
¼ teaspoon raw honey
2 cloves of garlic, peeled,
    minced
Dash of sea salt

Prepare artichoke by cutting off about a ¼ - ½-inch off the top. Using shears or kitchen scissors, trim the tips off of each leaf.

In a saucepan, fill the bottom with about an inch of water. Add lemon slices, garlic and 1 Bouquet Garni or 1 tablespoon Italian seasoning. Place a steamer basket on top of the water. Place artichokes into the basket. Cover. Bring to a boil. Reduce heat to a simmer, and continue steaming for 30 minutes, or until leaves become tender.

Sauce: In a small saucepan, melt butter over low heat. Remove from heat. Whisk in remaining ingredients.

Enjoy!

To eat an artichoke, pull a leaf off. The "meat" is at the bottom of each leaf. Dip it in your sauce and then pull it between your teeth to remove the desired part of the artichoke.

Crabby Cakes

This is just a simple crab cake recipe. Because these are void of breadcrumbs and filled with crabmeat, it's a looser crab cake. So, make sure you have a hot pan and small cakes ~ it makes it easier to flip!

16 ounces crabmeat
¼ cup almond meal
⅛ cup coconut flour
1 large egg
1 large shallot, finely diced
1 teaspoon sea salt
¼ teaspoon Old Bay® Seasoning
1 tablespoon horseradish
Bacon grease (or whatever oil you want to cook these in).
8 fresh lime wedges (from 2 limes)
Cocktail sauce (optional)

In a bowl, combine crabmeat, almond meal, coconut flour, egg, shallot, sea salt, Old Bay®, and horseradish. Refrigerate for 1 hour.

In a hot skillet, over medium-high heat, with a little bacon grease (this adds another layer of flavor), place mashed-down, golf-ball sized patties. Cook until browned on each side (about 3-4 minutes per side).

Transfer to a plate. Squeeze fresh lime over the patties and serve with homemade cocktail sauce (optional)!

Yield: 15-17 patties

Enjoy!

1 pound ground beef
½ green bell pepper, finely chopped
¼ teaspoon smoked paprika
½ teaspoon Italian seasoning
½ teaspoon garlic salt
½ teaspoon dry mustard
1 tablespoon pure maple syrup
6-ounce can organic tomato paste
Sea salt and ground pepper, to taste
Boston or Bibb lettuce leaves

In a 12-inch skillet, over medium heat, add ground beef, bell pepper, paprika, Italian seasoning, garlic salt, dry mustard, and maple syrup. Cook until beef is completely browned. Add tomato paste and stir. Cook an additional 5 minutes.

Add salt and pepper, to taste.

Fill lettuce leaves with meat filling. Eat like a soft taco.

Yield: 4-6 wraps, depending on the size of your lettuce cups

Enjoy!

Nutastic Dip

¼ cup raw pecans
½ cup raw almonds
1 tablespoons raw honey
1 tablespoon unsweetened
  applesauce
1 small banana

Optional: 2 tablespoons
unsweetened dried cherries (or
preferred fruit), finely diced

Place nuts in a food processor. Blend, forming a paste. Add honey, applesauce, and peeled banana. Blend, until smooth. Transfer into a bowl. Add dried fruit (optional).

Refrigerate, until ready to serve. Serve with celery sticks, apple slices, or whatever is in season!

Yield: approximately ¾ cup

Enjoy!

Fish Sticks

1 pound cod or halibut
1 cup pecan meal
   (or preferred nut meal
⅓ cup arrowroot
1 tablespoon fresh dill,
   chopped (dried dill is
   acceptable)
2 teaspoons sea salt
2 large eggs
Juice of 1 lime

Preheat oven to 350°F.

Cut cod/halibut into strips or "sticks".

Combine pecan meal, arrowroot, dill, and salt. Set aside.

Whisk eggs and lime juice. Set aside.

Line a baking sheet with parchment paper.

Dredge a piece of cod in egg mixture. Coat with the pecan meal mixture. Place on the parchment paper. Repeat with all cod/halibut pieces.

Bake 15 minutes, or when cod becomes opaque throughout.

Yield: 18-20 fish sticks

Enjoy!

Family Za Time!

Crust:
4 cups "riced" cauliflower
   (approximately 1 head)
eggs
1½ teaspoons sea salt
¼ cup almond meal
¼ teaspoon garlic powder
1½ tablespoons Italian
   seasoning

Topping Suggestions: Go wild!
A. Marinara sauce, basil,
   and yellow peppers
B. Pesto and Italian sausage
C. Marinara sauce, bacon,
   and onion
D. Pesto and mushrooms
E. Marinara sauce, black olive,
   and artichoke hearts

Preheat oven to 350°F.

"Rice" cauliflower by placing a chopped head of cauliflower in a blender with about 3 cups of water. Blend until the cauliflower resembles sticky rice. Transfer to a strainer. Take several paper towels and smoosh out the liquid from the cauliflower.

Combine cauliflower with remaining crust ingredients. On a parchment-lined baking sheet, form 10 crusts (approximately ¼ cup per crust). Bake 30 minutes.

Add desired toppings. Bake for an additional 5-10 minutes. Remove from oven. Cool, on baking sheet, 10 minutes. This will "harden" the crust.

Drizzle with olive oil, if desired.

Yield: 10 mini pizzas

Enjoy!

Pear Applesauce

4 pounds apples, any variety, peeled, cored and sliced
1 pound pears, any variety, peeled, cored and sliced
1 tablespoon ground cinnamon
⅛ cup water
Juice from 1 navel orange
¼ cup raw honey

Set your slow cooker to low heat and add all ingredients.

For the first two hours, stir about every 20 minutes, breaking the fruit down with your stirring spoon. Continue to cook 8 hours, or overnight.

If you like your applesauce completely smooth, use an immersion blender or regular blender to blend, after the allotted cooking time. Otherwise, break up the sauce with a spoon, to reach desired consistency.

Refrigerate, if not serving immediately. Just reheat if you prefer it warm.

Yield: approximately 5 cups

Enjoy!

Toasted Coconut Flakes

A very simple treat… great for a snack in the car!

1 coconut
2 tablespoons raw honey,
   slightly melted
¼ teaspoon sea salt

Preheat oven to 350°F.

Crack coconut and drain water into a bowl.

Chunk pieces of the coconut off of the shell. Place pieces into the coconut water, as you work. Once the coconut is completely chunked, strain.

Using a potato peeler, peel coconut flakes. Transfer to a clean bowl. Add honey and salt. Stir to evenly coat. Transfer to a parchment paper-lined baking dish and spread evenly.

Bake 20 minutes. Stir and flip every 5 minutes.

Turn oven off. Allow the coconut flakes to dry out, in the oven, for another 7 minutes.

Remove from oven. Cool 30 minutes.

Enjoy!

Cinnamon Pecan Crunch Cereal

This hits the mark (especially if you throw in a few dark chocolate chips, before serving)!

1 cup unsalted sunflower seeds

1 cup unsweetened coconut flakes

1 cup pecan pieces

2 tablespoons raw almond butter

¼ cup raw honey

⅛ cup coconut flour

⅛ cup pecan meal (ground pecans)

1 tablespoon ground cinnamon (my preference is Vietnamese Cinnamon ~ it has a "special" flavor that I love!)

Optional Toppings: dark chocolate chips, berries, banana slices

Preheat oven to 350°F.

Thoroughly combine all ingredients, in a bowl.
Press mixture evenly into greased 9x13 pan.
Bake 15-20 minutes, until browned. Cool 30 minutes.
Crumble into an airtight container, until ready to serve.

Enjoy!

Prosciutto e Melone

Ahhhh... this brings back great memories... as food should! Growing up a Navy Brat, we moved every few years, even months, sometimes! One of the best adventures was living in Naples, Italy. Italians know how to socialize around food ~ fantastic food, that is. The first time someone served me prosciutto wrapped around a honeydew melon slice, I thought they had lost their mind. However, it's just fantastic!! The saltiness and smokiness of the prosciutto wrapped around this sweet melon is a win.

6 slices of melon, rind removed
6 pieces of prosciutto

Wrap prosciutto slices around the melon at an angle.

If you are going to make melon ball bites, use 24 balls of melon. Quarter each prosciutto slice and wrap.

Enjoy!

For an appetizer, using a melon baller, ball the melons and wrap smaller strips of prosciutto around them. Skewer with a toothpick and watch them disappear as your guests devour them! This recipe is also great with mango!

Eggplant Dipping Sticks
with Honey BBQ Sauce

Eggplant:

1 small eggplant, peeled
    and sliced into sticks
    (½ inch thick)
2 large eggs
2 teaspoons prepared
    horseradish
1 cup almond meal
⅓ cup coconut flour
1 teaspoon fine sea salt

Sauce:

½ cup organic marinara
    (no added sugar)
¼ cup raw honey
¼ teaspoon Worcestershire
    sauce
⅛ teaspoon Sriracha
    (or preferred hot
    sauce)

Preheat oven to 400°F.

To prepare the eggplant, peel and discard skin. Cut into ½ –inch rounds. Slice each round into 4-5 sticks.

In one bowl, whisk together eggs and horseradish. In a larger, shallow bowl, combine almond meal, coconut flour, and sea salt.

Dredge each stick in the egg mixture and then coat with the dry mixture. Place each stick on a parchment paper-lined cookie sheet. Bake for approximately 20 minutes.

In a small saucepan, heat sauce ingredients to a low rolling boil. Cook for 5 minutes. Remove from heat.

Let sticks and sauce cool and then serve.

Serves 4

Enjoy!

You can control the chunkiness of your almond meal by making it yourself. I keep two containers of almond meal/flour in my pantry. In a food processor, blend your own raw, unsalted almonds, until desired consistency. I make a chunky version as well as a fine flour-like version. Depending on the recipe, I make my choice. You may find that you'll have a preference with different recipes.

Chicken & Waffles

To some, this may seem like a crazy combination, but there are many diners across the South that specialize in this delicacy. If you haven't before, I suggest you try it! If you have, just enjoy this down-home southern tradition!

Chicken:
3 large eggs
2 teaspoons yellow mustard
6 chicken legs
1 cup almond meal
¼ cup coconut flour
1 tablespoon Italian seasoning
1 teaspoon sea salt
½ teaspoon ground pepper

Waffles:
4 tablespoons organic, unsalted
    butter or ghee, softened
6 eggs
⅓ cup coconut flour
⅓ cup almond butter
1 small banana
1 teaspoon gluten free
    baking powder
1 teaspoon red pepper flakes
½ teaspoon ground celery seed
Pinch sea salt and ground pepper
Pure maple syrup

Preheat oven to 350°F.

In one bowl whisk 3 eggs. In another bowl, mix almond meal, Italian seasoning, salt and pepper.

Lightly oil a baking dish.

Dredge chicken legs in egg mixture and then coat with seasoned meal. Place in greased baking dish. Do this with each chicken leg. Bake 50-60 minutes, until internal temperature reaches 160°F (I use a meat thermometer) and the chicken is browned (Flip the chicken legs after 30 minutes of baking).

Preheat waffle iron. Blend butter, 6 eggs, coconut flour, almond butter, banana, baking powder, crushed red pepper flakes, ground celery seed, and a pinch each of salt & pepper.

Pour the appropriate amount of batter into waffle maker.

Serve chicken and waffles with a light drizzle of pure maple syrup.

Serves 6

Enjoy!

This recipe was made at the request of my girls. They haven't had fast-food chicken "yuck-its" (as they refer to them) in two years. My girls are great sports for trying all of my crazy creations. But every now and then, they just want something simple and "familiar".

2 large eggs
1 tablespoon yellow mustard
¾ cup almond flour
½ cup coconut flour
¼ cup arrowroot
1 tablespoon Italian seasoning
½ teaspoon sea salt
1 pound chicken tenders,
   cut in thirds

Honey Mustard:
¼ cup yellow mustard
¼ cup raw honey
2 teaspoons apple cider
   vinegar

Preheat oven to 350°F.

In one bowl, mix eggs and mustard. Whisk. Set aside.

In another bowl, mix almond flour, coconut flour, arrowroot, Italian seasoning, and sea salt.

Dip chicken parts in the wet mixture and then dredge in the dry ingredients. Place on a parchment paper-lined cookie sheet. Bake for 10 minutes. Flip chicken pieces.

Put under the broiler for an additional 7 minutes to continue to cook and allow to brown and crisp.

While the chicken is cooking, whisk together honey mustard ingredients. Set aside in the refrigerator. Serve chicken with the dip.

Serves 4

Enjoy!

Banana Fudge Pops

2 small ripe bananas
¾ cup coconut milk
¼ cup unsweetened cocoa powder
1 teaspoon raw honey
¼ teaspoon banana extract
    (optional)

With a hand mixer or blender, blend all ingredients, until smooth. Pour into preferred molds.

Freeze overnight. Serve.

Enjoy!

Pure vanilla can be substituted for the banana extract. My youngest daughter doesn't like coconut milk. However, I find that just a little extract helps mask the coconut flavor. It's a completely optional ingredient.

Dark Chocolate & Almond Butter Fondue, with Apples

This is just a quick and easy snack that can be used with whatever fruit you have in the house ~ great not only with apples, but also with banana slices, pitted cherries and peaches.

3 ounces dark chocolate
   (72% or higher)
¼ cup almond butter, creamy

Apple slices, pitted cherries, banana slices, peaches, or whatever you want to dip into chocolate!

In a double boiler, over medium-low heat, melt chocolate and almond butter, until smooth.

If you are civilized, transfer this mixture to a fondue pot; however, my family and I knocked this back in five minutes flat!

Enjoy!

 If you do not have a double boiler, all you need is a pot and a metal bowl. Pour about a 1-inch level of water into the pot. Place metal bowl on top, without the bowl touching the water. Your chocolate will go in the bowl.

Apple-Spiced Caramel-Dipped Doughnuts

Doughnuts:
3 Medjool dates, pitted and finely chopped
¼ cup coconut flour
½ teaspoon gluten free baking powder
2 cups apples, peeled, cored and finely chopped
5 large eggs
Pinch of sea salt
½ teaspoon vanilla extract
½ teaspoon cinnamon
½ teaspoon ground allspice
¼ cup creamy almond butter

Caramel Dip:
7 ounces coconut milk
⅛ teaspoon baking soda
2 tablespoons ghee or organic, unsalted butter
Pinch of sea salt
⅛ teaspoon butter extract
½ teaspoon vanilla
1 tablespoons raw honey
¼ teaspoons cinnamon
¼ cup organic coconut palm sugar

In a mixing bowl, blend doughnut ingredients until well-blended (this will be a slightly chunky batter). Fill the bottom half of the doughnut maker until level. Lower top half and cook for approximately 3-4 minutes until firm and slightly browned. Let cool on a cooling rack. Continue to cook until batter is gone.

For the caramel: Place ingredients in a medium saucepan. Heat to a boiling for 4 minutes. Continue to cook for approximately 30 minutes on low, stirring often. The sauce will darken and thicken. Cook until it thickly coats your spoon.

Dip the tops of the doughnuts in the sauce and place on a cooling rack. Refrigerate.

Yield: 18-20 mini doughnuts

Enjoy!

Notes

Index

Index

CPSIA information can be obtained
at www.ICGtesting.com
Printed in the USA
LVIC06n1008190214
374089LV00006BA/14

9 780982 548080